The *LION*
Attitude

Reinventing Leadership Development

for Architects, Engineers, and Construction Professionals (AEC)

KIRBY LEE

ISBN: 979-8-9909616-0-9 (Paperback)
ISBN: 979-8-9909616-1-6 (Hardcover)
ISBN: 979-8-9909616-2-3 (eBook)

Library of Congress Control Number: 2024913213

Printed in Apex, North Carolina, USA by Kirby Lee.

Photo credit for headshot or other images and graphics inside the book: Dan Halpern, Tara Lee, and Peak City Headshots.

The publisher has strived to be as accurate and complete as possible in the creation of this book.

For more information, visit www.LionAttitude.com.

For bulk book orders, contact Kirby Lee at Kirby@LionAttitude.com.

Dedication

This book is dedicated to the Architecture/Engineering/Construction (AEC) community that does so much of the unseen work that our society needs to be able to function. Our work is usually taken for granted by society, but I know how much of an I+M+P+A+C=T we make in the world. My goal behind this book is to create a better place for the AEC world so it can thrive for more generations to come and become the premier industry that people want to be part of.

To my Mom and Dad: It took a long time for me to find my way and my purpose for being on this earth. Thank you for being there along the journey as the model of the blue-collar hard work that I needed in my life.

Your Bonus Gift – The Lion Attitude Toolkit

Thank you for joining me in the mission of reinventing leadership in the Architecture/Engineering/Construction industry (AEC). From the content inside *The Lion Attitude*, you discover a much clearer understanding of how to move forward with your own leadership growth.

Let's walk together as you are expanding your leadership skills. I'll be with you, rooting for your success every step of the way.

To help you move forward faster on this new journey toward masterful leadership in all areas of your life, I've created a special gift for you.

The *Lion Attitude Toolkit* includes the resources I found invaluable as I was going through my own leadership reinvention. This list includes websites, useful tools, motivational speeches, and other information I used during my journey to reinvent myself, and ultimately create a training system designed to address the particular challenges of AEC leadership development.

I hope you find these resources as meaningful as I did. The toolkit will be expanded and updated as I discover even more information and ideas to help you.

Just go to www.LionAttitude.com/bonustoolkit and tell me where to send it.

Remember we are here to win together. Welcome to the lion pride!

Kirby

Table of Contents

Introduction

The Lion Awakens

The topic of leadership development comes up frequently in conversations in the Architecture/Engineering/Construction (AEC) space, with increasing importance. We're faced with an ever-changing landscape of technology, new regulations, and business model adjustments. AEC is a field full of very technical and blue-collar roots, given that our industry is at the very heart of how buildings come to life. We need to change the way we teach leadership if we want our industry to thrive into the future.

I come from three generations of HVAC contractors. I practiced engineering in the AEC space for eighteen years before switching over into an owner's representative role for the government. Then I moved on into HVAC equipment sales. Regardless of all the different sub-areas of AEC I worked in, the topic of seeing poor leadership firsthand never seemed to go away.

Unfortunately, my big dreams of staying at an engineering company and becoming a principal faded away. During my career I heard the frustrations of others in our industry and also personally experienced the poor general policy of promoting people based primarily on their technical ability and not their skills as a leader of others.

Over the course of my career, these poorly trainer leaders were great individual technical craftsmen in their field. Unfortunately, they didn't get leadership training or support, which resulted in constant turnover and low morale. This caused my energy levels to drain over the course of my career.

Why would something that I wanted to do my whole life suddenly feel like an energy suck I didn't want to bear anymore?

I think the best analogy I could think of back then was a Lion being locked up in its cage, left to slumber for a very long time.

Taking a very deep look back on my AEC career, there was simply one thing in common every time:

Poor leadership development in the AEC space by technical professionals

I can attest to this firsthand with my experience working for engineering firms. There was basically no leadership development at all once I started to manage people. The automatic assumption is that if you are a great AEC technical professional, then you should move into a leadership role. This applies to architects and contractors as well. I know because I've talked to many over the years. After you get promoted with zero to little training, you realize leading people is not the same as being a technical professional in the AEC industry.

When leadership development is offered by AEC companies, it's not relevant. Unfortunately, in nearly every case, the trainer and program that is taught to an AEC professional always comes from outside, provided by people with no experience or background in our field.

These trainers assume that the design and construction field is just like every other industry they are used to working with. It's not. They don't understand that teaching leadership to technical AEC professionals requires addressing unique industry issues.

Corporate America would like everything in leadership development to be a simple linear process, just like they are used to experiencing. Well, I am here to throw a bucket of cold water on their assumed reality by saying this has been ineffective in the design and construction field.

The AEC industry is a very complex and dynamic field, with things constantly on the move when it comes to construction. There are issues occurring daily that are 99% of the time outside of your control, regardless of how much planning you try to do as an AEC professional. Great examples of this include weather delays, moving target supply chain deliveries on equipment, owner and design changes, labor issues, and the list keeps on going.

Do you know how many projects go according to a schedule on either the design or construction side in the field? I can tell you from my years of experience that it never happens according to the day one plan, and usually takes longer than expected.

Clearly, the AEC industry faces a lot of future staffing issues with declining interest in STEM and construction. In addition, older people are retiring while younger ones are leaving the field completely, creating more shortages. AEC companies are always saying, "We are hiring and can never find good people." This issue can be traced back to the lack of leadership development in our industry.

But how are we going to solve these issues that the AEC industry I love so much faces with needed leadership development for the next generation?

The only way we can address this is by implementing a specialized leadership development system that is designed for our industry and built with an understanding of the unique challenges AEC professionals and businesses face every day.

The process of the Lion Attitude is a leadership development system built to be a long-term solution that will take time to understand and implement. It's specifically designed for the AEC industry. Developing leadership talent from the ground up isn't a quick fix. It's time to stop implementing temporary fixes. Doing so turns out just as poorly as the results that come from AEC professionals who try to take shortcuts as part of their craft, hoping for a cheap and easy solution.

Now is the time for the AEC industry to start cleaning up our industry leadership problems from the ground up.

I invite and welcome you on a journey to be part of a movement to change the AEC industry. Together, we can make this a field that people want to be part of for many generations after we leave this earth. It won't be an easy journey, but I am here to walk side-by-side with you as part of the process to reinvent how we develop leadership skills for our field.

Having stronger leadership skills in the AEC industry allows for leaders and organizations to benefit in the following ways:

- Attract and retain employees
- Increase productivity among team members
- Create higher profits
- Reduce turnover
- Develop a stronger company culture

The Lion Attitude is a specialized AEC leadership development system built in phases like what we see on construction sites and in design documents. Read through each of the phases in order and carefully work to follow the steps of the system in order from Phase One to Phase Four. The book is designed to ensure a person has strong inner self-leadership first, before they start working on leadership development for managing others.

After all, you can't be good at leading others if you don't know how to lead yourself first, right?

Phases One and Two provide the process to develop and strengthen purpose as part of an individual's inner self-leadership. Phases Three and Four cover the application of purpose while developing your leadership outwards by learning how to Act + Connect at the same time.

Let's begin with the most important part of the journey in Phase One with the steps to develop purpose.

Phase One

Inner Leadership – Reinvention & Purpose Development

Before we get started on the journey through Phase One, I'd like to cover a few things to help bring you the most value from this book as an AEC professional. Let me start by answering two questions. Then we'll begin your reinvention journey.

Why is this book called The Lion Attitude?

Lions are one of the most fascinating animals in the world. They are rare animals capable of doing things that leave us as humans in complete awe of these special creatures. They operate fearlessly, executing a strategy in a way where prey never sees a lion coming until it's too late. Lion prides also work in teams, hunting animals with flawless precision. Then they take their spoils back to the pride, so all the family members can eat together in triumph.

Lions are also one of the most social animals in the world, demonstrating mastery of connection with others. Their ability to connect is unmatched as they can build lasting long-term relationships, master their emotions, and work daily to communicate, growing their social skills.

When we think of lions, the first attributes that come to mind are courage, strength, bravery, leadership, and heart.

You can see that lions use these attributes to master action and connection, which is a very rare combination in the wild. All of this sounds amazing, right? We should all want to exhibit the lion's behavior in our leadership development. After all, lions are kings of the jungle for a reason. They're masters of everything in their lives.

If we act like lions in every way, we can make a significant impact in the AEC community. Together, we can reduce or eliminate the struggles people in our industry face daily in offices and on construction jobsites such as:

- Attracting talent in the AEC industry (which has a labor shortage to begin with).
- Reduced mental health concerns and preventing burnout.
- Retaining talent and preventing key workers exit to other industries.

What does successful leadership development look like in the AEC industry?

Using lion terminology, I see successful leadership as getting down to some basic math equations we can all understand. Below are two I'll use throughout the book:

Phase 1 & 2 (Inner Leadership): Intention + Motivation = Purpose

Phase 3 & 4 (Outer Leadership): Intention + Motivation + Purpose + Action + Connection = Triumph (I+M+P+A+C=T)

When I look at people who embody successful leadership development, and specifically mentors in my life, I see the I+M+P+A+C=T (IMPACT) when having discussions with people in my inner lion pride circle.

Our goal in developing leadership skills is to create IMPACT on everything we touch and with the people we serve. Developing leadership is not an easy task as an AEC professional trying to balance technical skills and helping people get better at their job at the same time. Lions are rare animals for a reason. Successful impactful leadership is also a very rare thing.

You can see in looking at the first math equation that purpose is important, but it's based on a formula that you need to be intentional and motivated to develop it. You will often hear that you may accidentally fall into your purpose one day. My opinion and observation is that people try to find their purpose, but it takes dedicated effort toward a specific goal to be in the right position to capture it like lions do in the wild.

You can't develop leadership skills if you have no purpose or direction. Think of this as driving a car without a GPS, stranded in the middle of nowhere with no data to draw from to know how you ended up there to begin with. What are your chances of getting to a destination you want to travel? I have that answer for you . . . ZERO.

You can develop purpose by simply applying the **Intention + Motivation = Purpose** equation to your life. It's required for your leadership development. However, you must put in the work to make it a reality and be motivated to keep going, even when things are hard. Leadership is not for the faint of heart. It's a major responsibility. If you have built a strong purpose, you will be able to make it as a leader in the AEC industry.

If you don't have a strong purpose, you will not create any impact. Any AEC technical professional should be able to visually see how the math breaks down in this equation. Ultimately, strong leadership is being built from within to develop and keep purpose strong.

Now let's look at the second equation, or I+M+P+A+C=T (IMPACT), where outer leadership comes into play.

The back half of the math shows once you have developed your purpose in an unbreakable manner like a lion, the time comes to apply it in the real world by learning how to Act + Connect. Note that I am saying act AND connect, not act OR connect. Successful leadership in the AEC industry is based on action and connection together.

Notice how lions are elite animals as masters of action and connection, using both at the same time. The math shows you that doing both together with purpose creates triumphs and wins all around for yourself as a leader and for others.

Putting this all together you can see that lions are specialists at all the six words spelling I+M+P+A+C=T. This is our goal with leadership development for ourselves too.

Our goal is to create IMPACT on everything we touch, including the people around us, in a positive way.

Let's start on the first phase of the journey, the reinvention of everything so you can work to develop your purpose in building strong inner leadership.

Chapter 1

Reinventing Yourself

This chapter is really the most challenging part of the journey. The best way I like to describe this journey toward developing yourself is starting to look at leadership as coming from within.

The time is now to take a deep hard look at yourself to see what IMPACT you want to make for yourself and others around you. I call this moment "rock bottom," since you start to deeply reflect on how you got to this point to begin with. This is the part of the journey where you start to look at yourself in the mirror to see who you really are in your leadership development.

This look in the mirror is not an easy thing to swallow. That moment I realized I was doing everything wrong as a leader was honestly the most painful moment I have faced. But the good thing about the rock-bottom phase of reinventing yourself is that you can only move up from there.

During this phase, reinventing yourself means you must be ready to let go of all the things you have learned in the past so this new person developing leadership skills as an AEC professional can come to the surface. This journey through The Lion Attitude and all the phases is a hard walk that is not for the faint of heart.

But as in life, the hardest and longest walks lead to the greatest destinations. The goal of reinvention is seeing your leadership efforts develop into you becoming a person you can be proud of at the end of the book. In addition to yourself, you will be affecting others in a positive way. It will be clear how much IMPACT you will have on the AEC industry as well.

The reinvention and future steps will result in a lot of knock downs in the process, which isn't going to feel very good. Moments of failure along the way are something we all encounter, but they are meant to be lessons to teach you how to move forward and become better.

Remember these words as you make your first steps:

You will be knocked down developing your leadership skills but don't ever be knocked out.

The Journey & Steps to Reinvention

Let's walk through the very early steps to get you some quick wins and a feeling of confidence as an AEC professional working to develop your leadership.

Step One – Find a very quiet place where you can be alone for extended periods of time for at least a couple of hours. This is a place you will likely be visiting in the future as you continue the journey to develop leadership skills built through the Lion Attitude. For me it was a park bench at Lake Pine, which overlooks the water in Apex, NC. This is where I have lived most of my life as an adult.

Step Two – Take a note pad or something you can write on like a tablet and put into words what you are feeling right now about how you got to this point. If you can, I would recommend avoiding music or media while sitting and letting your thoughts flow into something you can visualize. It's interesting what enters your mind when you can sit in silence thinking to yourself.

Step Three – Now that you have really gotten into a state of deep reflection, let's start answering the questions below to peel open the inner layers of yourself:

Are you currently feeling successful, happy, and fulfilled professionally?

Do you have the complete support of leadership above you at work to develop your own leadership skills?

What is the current state of your overall physical, mental, and emotional health and well-being right now?

How do you feel when you wake up each day thinking about yourself overall and professionally?

Do you feel grateful and excited about all the things that happen each day?

Do you feel you create IMPACT on people? Do you get this feedback from others and what do they tell you?

What do you see the best version of yourself looking like right now and in a year going forward?

What most people will encounter at this point is that they are not where they want to be in life in every aspect. I read a statistic by Gallup (workforce employee engagement surveys) showing 75% of people in the workforce are unhappy with their jobs in some way, shape, or form due to lack of purpose.

The AEC industry takes this to another level, with labor shortage issues in all areas and an older generation workforce getting ready to retire.

This leaves a massive opportunity for people to come into the industry and create IMPACT on the world now and for generations to come.

When I began this journey, I was honestly in that 75%, and was ready to walk away from all of it for good. This was even after working on my leadership development to grow my career.

But once you get around the tough exterior of the AEC industry, you realize these are salt of the earth people doing everything they can to make the world a better place. None of the other vertical markets are even possible without Architects/Engineers/Contractors making things a reality with their technical abilities and problem-solving skills.

And I saved the last step of the process for after all this reflection:

Make sure that how you feel in this moment is something you remember for the rest of your days moving forward. Expect this to be very emotional. It was for me, realizing just how unhappy I was with how I answered every one of those questions.

> **Your goal from this point forward is to fight every day like a lion for this new person you want to be and to never feel like you do at this point again.**

Application Example: Sally's Reinventing Yourself Moment

I met someone a while back who was a younger AEC professional named Sally. When I was meeting people at this office for the first time on a visit, the team manager pointed out Sally specifically. The manager told me Sally was trying to find her way and had been around for a few years.

On one of the days during my visit, we had a little down time and went out to lunch together at PF Chang's. I knew Sally a little bit before my visit. We had communicated here and there working on projects together.

During our lunch conversation, Sally told me how much she was struggling in her role. I started talking to her about purpose and the process of Intention + Motivation that creates it, sharing my story from the past. She had come from a technical engineering background and mentioned how much she liked being in the AEC industry.

Then I asked Sally a question.

"Sally, why are you doing this job and what makes you want to keep doing this on a daily basis?"

Sally responded with a blank stare. She looked at me for several minutes thinking about this powerful statement. I could tell she was thinking of some reason to respond back. The response that came out of her mouth is something I will never forget.

"Kirby, I honestly have no idea why I am doing this job anymore."

In this moment, Sally was hit by a major realization. Sally was in the 75% who lacked purpose and it was showing in all her struggles. She didn't have the Intention + Motivation behind why she was doing the job. Everyone around her, and even Sally, was seeing the ultimate result of lack of purpose.

After that lunch conversation, I remember telling Sally about how she could reinvent herself that day. Sally said she needed some time to work on herself to really understand the direction she wanted to travel.

There were internal organizational opportunities I knew about and I shared a little bit about them with her. Sally seemed really energized talking about some specific roles we went through. I referred her to some people who could give her more details about the jobs. The goal behind this discussion was to get Sally to see what she really wanted to do with her life. Ultimately, Sally needed to go on this journey to discover herself and what her purpose was in this moment.

As part of this process, she had to obtain manager approval for a transfer. I asked Sally's manager how she was doing on the team and if he would support her if she wanted to take on a new role.

The manager said something like:

"Sally needs to spend some more time in her current role. She isn't ready for a new role."

This was disappointing to hear. There was a clear disconnect between Sally and her manager. Sally's purpose was eroding over time. The manager was not thinking about what was best for his employee. I knew when the manager made this statement it was likely going to be the end of the relationship for both in the future. "Rock bottom" had arrived for both sides.

Two months later, when I was scrolling on LinkedIn, I saw this message:

"Congrats to Sally for taking a new role at . . ."

I vividly remember reaching out to Sally afterwards. She said our lunch conversation made her decide to take a week of vacation time to reflect. She determined she wanted to travel professionally. She also acknowledged our lunch conversation helped her recognize how bad she felt.

When Sally came back to work, she knew with clarity that things needed to be different going forward. What exactly would come after "rock bottom" was not clear to her, but there was going to be something different happening in Sally's life.

She decided to leave that job and take a position that allowed her to go further in her career. Sally has been at that job ever since. She told me that lunch conversation changed everything.

Sally's story is a great example of how someone can reinvent themselves from a very low point. It all goes back to the math equation again:

Intention + Motivation = Purpose

Can you see how Sally's rock-bottom moment led her to realize she was missing purpose? Notice Sally's inner leadership was kicking in saying it was time to find her purpose. She created it by being motivated and intentional, which is a function of inner leadership development.

So now we'll move forward into the next step of Purpose Development.

Chapter 2

Purpose Development & Discovery

It's time to make your first steps forward to develop purpose. I'll be walking with you, traveling on the journey to develop your inner leadership in this important step. The key to all of this is making sure you are focused on the words Intention + Motivation during Phase One. Your purpose isn't going to happen if you don't put in the effort to capture it like a lion hunting its prey in the wild.

Questions that come up during this process include:

Is it possible to seek your purpose?

Can't you just simply walk into your purpose?

How do you know when you find purpose?

What is the feeling like when you have purpose?

What next step do you take when you find purpose?

The topic of purpose led me to an insatiable curiosity about what motivates those who are successful as leaders in the AEC industry. I was surprised by what I discovered:

Many come from nothing just like me.

There is always someone who has fewer skills than you have in your current leadership development. Here are some areas you may want to develop:

Passion, Money, Resources, Relationships, Intelligence, Opportunities

The most successful leaders in the AEC industry had to work their way up every step of the way. Our field is all tied to professional licensure, so you're required to have practical experience before stepping into a role where you are responsible for supervising the work of others. This should inspire you when you look at where you want to go as a professional leader.

Someone has already done this before you started the process. You are not the first person to accomplish anything in this field as a leader.

This concept felt like a moment of freedom in my mind. The weight of all my previous failures in leadership development was starting to fall off. The logic is simple. When you put in the same work and effort on yourself, you can reach your leadership development goals while making a large impact on the AEC industry in the long run.

Think of how many people became millionaires who were self-made and came from nothing. One of my favorite speakers is Eric Thomas. He was homeless and lived in abandoned buildings, eating out of trash cans during his early years. It took him twelve years to get a bachelor's degree from Michigan State University. This sounds rough. You would never wish this on a human being. Eric is now famous worldwide as a motivational speaker who talks to professional and college sports teams.

This is an illustration of just how powerful purpose is. You can bet that Eric was intentionally motivated to fight daily for the life he wanted. Lions also have this level of intention and motivation. We as leaders need to have this as well to be successful in our development.

Steps to Purpose Development & Discovery

Most people in life are not born into wealth, success, or extreme luck. This is where the reinvention starts: by building yourself from the ground up. We all have this lion inside ourselves waiting to be unleashed on the world.

People with purpose find a way to keep moving forward, even in the worst of times. Right after I found my purpose, it was tested with the new department director in my boring government job. My role was changed without any input from me. And, while those circumstances were not great, it was the reason I got to this point of telling you this story. I could have easily rolled over, just like in the past, but something in me was different. I didn't understand what at the time. It was the lion inside me awakening and wanting to break out of its cage, determined to not let my life continue the way it was.

My personal development journey led me to study every single aspect of lion behavior. My focus was on lion traits, hunting habits, interacting with other members of the pride, and social structure, among other things. Lions spend their entire lives focused on hunting. They have a purpose like no other animal in the world. It is this trait that allows them to focus only on the things that matter and not waste time on anything that doesn't align with being a master hunter.

People who have a purpose in life can hunt just like lions do in the wild. They have a clear vision of exactly what they want, how they are going to get it, and all the steps that need to be mastered to achieve their goals.

Purpose allows you to keep going when many of the "sheep" quit as things get hard. And purpose allows you to perform at levels that you could only imagine prior to such focus.

A quote from the Fearless Motivation speech "Purpose" says, "There is nothing more powerful than a human being with purpose."

So, let's start the steps toward finding your purpose…

Step One – Minimal Radio and TV time

This sounds like a major surprise, but I want to ask a question:

How much impact does catching re-runs of a *Friends* episode on TV have on your future?

As you would expect, re-runs of *Friends* will not change your future. That shouldn't sound like a major shocker. Ever notice how Lions are laser-focused and, as a result, accomplish amazing things as leaders?

It's time to minimize your distractions and give yourself time to focus on this important aspect of the journey toward developing your leadership abilities. It's amazing how much you can figure out just by sitting in silence. Give yourself time to reflect on problems and see ways to turn your future around.

If sitting in your house with no TV or radio is not an option, a great place to start could be going to a remote part of a park and sitting in nature. There was a great place that had a bench overlooking the water on Lake Johnson in Raleigh, NC. I remember going there in college at night, just to look at the moon on the water. I made so many decisions in my life at this spot. Of course, it's interesting that I didn't go there during one of the toughest times in my life when I was driven to "reinvention" awareness, but alas, that is the way the universe played out for me.

Step Two – Motivational & Inspirational Speeches

The quickest way to find your mission and purpose is to simply go out and hunt for it like lions do in the wild. The way I found mine was listening to speeches on websites like Fearless Motivation or Fearless Soul. This website is among many places where you can go through endless amounts of material covering all types of speaking styles and topics. Some speakers are more intense with a focus on motivation, while others are a little more serene or cerebral.

You can also look up podcast speeches to download on any phone, tablet, or computer for free or with a music service subscription. Lots of great websites exist to help guide you through mission and purpose discovery. I've mentioned Fearless Motivation and Fearless Soul as a couple of my favorites, but you should find what speaks to you.

My recommendation is to listen to a lot of speeches of all different types. I promise that something will call you over time. It might not be like what I found to develop my mission, but at some point, if you are sitting in silence listening to material like this, it will lead you to finding something that makes your heart jump to where inspiring words come out of your mouth.

Step Three – Celebrate This Special Moment

Tears rolled down my face the day I uttered the words that formed the purpose of how I was going to work on developing my leadership skills.

There is something special about this day when you discover your purpose statement. It's something that can't ever be taken from you for the rest of your life.

We hear stories all the time about championship teams that won in sports. The stories are often about the journey it took to get there. Think of this moment like the day the Carolina Hurricanes won the Stanley Cup in 2006. My wife and I were fortunate enough to be in the PNC Arena for game seven of the Stanley Cup playoffs. I remember watching the look on Rod Brind'Amour's face as he was coming to pick up the Stanley Cup that night. All the players were crying and celebrating the journey toward this special point.

I knew something was different. After I developed my purpose, something was different in me that I can never fully explain in words. I felt more accomplished than I had with anything I had accomplished before, personally or professionally. Based on how strongly I felt back then, I knew I was never going to go back to the person I was before and was going to make more substantial, positive changes in my life.

And nothing was going to stop me from developing my leadership skills in a way that would have an impact on everyone and everything around me.

Application Example: Kirby's Purpose Development & Discovery

June 27, 2019, was a day that I will never forget.

I was in the middle of a three-day training class being taught on Steven Covey's 7 Habits of Highly Effective People. At the time I was working in a government job as an owner's representative after my career switch from AEC consulting engineering.

In the beginning, I felt this was going to help me with my leadership role in the upcoming year with ASHRAE (American Society of Heating Air Conditioning Refrigeration Engineers).

I was preparing for a full year term as President of the Triangle Chapter in the Raleigh-Duram, NC area that started on July 1st, 2019. During this year I was going to be leading a team of volunteers that would be putting on an entire schedule of events. This Covey training was going to be a key component of how I was going to successfully lead the team to serve our membership.

During the last day of the class, the instructor mentioned how one of the final steps of the Covey process was the development of a Purpose Statement. At that point I was thinking about all the questions I highlighted above.

"Kirby, how are you going to find your purpose out of all this training?"

In my head I was going back to the origins of my switch from engineering to owner's representative. I wasn't enjoying the job during the last few years of my career in consulting engineering.

My current owner's rep role had me energized again. I was excited to be part of the government working for a department director who was a civil engineer. He understood the engineering mindset and knew I was an asset with my expertise in HVAC systems and Energy Modeling. It was the first time in a while I felt like someone wanted me to be part of something that was a big opportunity.

The next day after the training ended, my wife and my little baby girl were heading to Pennsylvania to see her parents. Typically, she would go up there during the summer for a week. I would stay behind at the house by myself focused on work, since I usually didn't have enough time off if I wanted to save it for Christmas.

Something inside me said this was an opportunity to think about my Purpose Statement. I was heavily focused on making this a priority. Looking back, this was my Intention + Motivation subconsciously at work. It was almost like the universe gave me this alone time in 2019 to think about my purpose.

On the first evening alone, I could not get this Purpose Statement out of my mind. The constant reflection that evening pulled me into a phrase I would say while I was at one of my past engineering firms:

"Let the lion out of the cage!"

That statement had me looking up a ton of lion quotes to see if there was something that inspired me. I found many sources of motivational speeches regarding lion behavior. Then I saved them to my playlist to listen to on the drive home from work. I was hoping one would catch my interest.

I found my purpose. It hit me when I listened to a specific speech regarding lion mentality by Chris Ross. The words brought chills to me. I remember pulling into a parking lot on Cary Parkway as the speech came on in my Chevy Cobalt.

"Everyone has the heart of a lion inside of them...let it out!"

I remember hearing that Chris Ross speech and knowing something was different inside me. For the first time I heard words that resonated with me as I envisioned who I wanted to be. There was something about the lion that was calling me. I could feel it inside me awakening from the slumber in the cage.

Looking back, it was the Intention + Motivation that generated my ability to find my purpose. I spent over a week at that house by myself in deep reflection looking for answers. I started listening to speeches and anything I could to find that spoke to me. My sole focus was finding purpose no matter what.

When I got home, I cried as I listened to this speech repeatedly throughout the evening. For the first time I felt like I found something that represented me and the newly reinvented person I wanted to be. I had a path forward to open the door to the cage and let the lion out.

My Purpose Statement became the words: **Courage, Strength, Bravery, Leadership, & Heart**

When I uttered those words, I felt a sense of power that I had never felt before. I knew that everything in my life from that moment needed to be based on those five things. I also knew if I didn't follow those five areas, I would continue into a life I was living but didn't want anymore.

Phase One is about purpose. Intention + Motivation are the key components for generating purpose. At the same time, you're working on developing and building inner leadership to move forward in a new direction.

Purpose is something you are trying to seek out. It's not going to fall into your lap. Next we'll work on building a Purpose Statement. This is easier to see once the lion is awakened. It's something you can embody as part of your inner leadership development.

Chapter 3

Purpose Branding & Embodiment

When I was developing purpose for myself to be a better leader, it didn't occur to me to write it down in a place where I could see it in a permanent form. In the business world, we all know verbal agreements don't mean anything. Written agreements and contracts that clearly articulate a scope of work with commitments on deliverables is how the business world works.

Think of it as producing a business agreement for yourself to follow your purpose that has been developed. Written contracts are important in our field. Think of this leadership development work as the same concept.

> **Writing a Purpose Statement down on a piece of paper or some other permanent form is a critical step to your success.**

We see so many people in life talk a great game about all the things they want. I discovered the idea of a vision board by listening to the famous Steve Harvey giving a speech on YouTube called "Write the Vision." I know what you are thinking, Steve Harvey is a celebrity and does all those shows on TV, including *Family Feud*. He's had life handed to him.

To all the people who think Steve had it easy in life, this is far from the truth. *Steve Harvey was homeless for several years, went bankrupt, had a severe stuttering problem as a child, and was divorced multiple times. Steve was told as a child by his schoolteacher he would never be on TV. When Steve told people he wanted to go into comedy, he was laughed at by many people, but was always working on himself with this vision he had in his head.*

In the "Write the Vision" speech, Steve has a powerful message that refers to a biblical verse he paraphrases:

"Write the vision and make it plain, so that he who reads it shall run toward it. And tarry (take a long time) for surely it will come at its appointed time."

Many have talked about the power of vision boards. Biblical verses tell us about the importance of writing things down. Simply thinking about doing things isn't enough. We need to commit in a tangible form.

There is a name for ideas in our head that aren't written down. They are called wishes…and wishes rarely become reality.

Now let's walk through the steps on this part of the Phase One process.

Step One – Write Down Your Purpose Statement

Head to your quiet place mentioned in Chapter Two and carry a notebook with you to start writing down words or ideas that come out of the discovery process. Being able to visualize the words is a powerful act, especially after hearing them spoken in a way that resonates with you through your discovery progression.

When you find your purpose and can put this into words, it is a pivotal moment. There is a lot of work done to get to this point, so make sure you write this down and just look at it for a couple of days.

How does it feel reading this statement right now?

Does your energy level rise when you say the words?

Can you look in the mirror saying this to yourself?

What type of facial and body expressions happen when you do this?

Your Purpose Statement will be something you carry with you for the rest of your days on this earth as part of your new path to leadership development. The purpose formed will be your north star you can always rely on in the best and worst of times during your leadership development.

Here are some exercise questions to consider after this pivotal moment, which are important to vet to see how powerful your statement really is for moving forward.

Exercise Questions

Is your Purpose Statement powerful enough to say when you look at yourself in the mirror when you wake up in the morning? And believe it?

Is your Purpose Statement powerful enough you can say it on your worst days when life has handed you some terrible cards? Can you create a mind shift that gets you back on track for positive outcomes?

Are you committed to following your Purpose Statement even if you must do this alone?

Are you willing to follow your Purpose Statement when people tell you it's not possible or no one else can see it?

If you can answer all these questions with a yes and there is ZERO hesitation every time, you are on your way. Your reinvention is coming along very well.

I remember the very first time I uttered the words of my Purpose Statement and wrote it down in front of my eyes. My purpose development happened during the last week of June 2019. I took advantage of my wife and daughter being out of town visiting family, leaving me behind to be on my own for a week.

During this week, there was a moment when I was looking in my bathroom mirror alone in my week of isolation. My goal behind looking in that mirror was developing an Intention that I was going to find my purpose behind developing my leadership skills. I was also motivated to make it a reality and was not going to walk out of that week without something that made me feel alive for the first time.

I don't know what it feels like to be a lion in real life, but they are clearly very powerful creatures in the wild. Something about looking in the mirror and proudly uttering the words was an experience that I can't explain even to this very day: **Courage, Strength, Bravery, Leadership, Heart.**

It's something even today, nearly five years later, that I still do even on the worst of days.

Step Two – Purpose Statement Embodiment

During this step in the process, focus on taking this powerful process of your purpose developed into a physical form. Think of this part to develop a stronger connection in a physical way and to have something to keep with you as you work on your purpose activities.

I started looking up ways to buy personalized and reasonably priced items I could wear on me or keep on my person. I started to visualize what the text of my message would look like and how all the words looked together. To take steps even further, I had a customized art drawing made with my branding font and the words of my purpose proudly displayed.

There was something powerful about the day all this personalized stuff arrived. I was moved so much by seeing it that I was in tears for a while. I knew I was going to wear my mission on me for the rest of my life. There was no way I was ever going to sway from it, even during tough times in the future.

Here is what I recommend in this step that will be key for your purpose embodiment:

Invest in personalized silicone bands or something cheap you can carry or wear on you even at night. The bands I bought were waterproof, so I could even wear them in the shower or on the beach or while swimming.

I recommend not spending more than $25 to $50 at a site like Reminderband. You can get keychains, dog tags, or bracelets in hundreds of different fonts and colors. The artwork design I created and had put on a canvas was right at around $100 back then, so you can see this isn't a large sum of money we are talking about. The goal isn't to go broke over your purpose.

Step Three – Taking Total Responsibility for your Purpose Statement

Some of the motivational material I was consuming mentioned this concept called Total Responsibility as part of my development toward working out on my final journey to lose weight.

I can't even remember the speaker, to be honest, but the concept is born out of this idea that every person is totally responsible for every aspect of their life. My first thoughts listening to this speech entered my head:

"Is this person crazy? Am I totally responsible for all aspects of my life? How is this possible?"

The speech gave an example of how someone decided to go drinking at night and stayed out at a bar very late. This person is an adult. There was nothing illegal in the eyes of the law with this decision. After a night of drinking, they leave the bar and make their way home. Unfortunately, they have an 8 a.m. meeting the next day with a key client and have a presentation to work on.

The person gets up after very little sleep for this meeting with the client and isn't focused. The key client can tell something is off. Because of the poor performance in this meeting and presentation, the client decides to take their business elsewhere.

In the normal world someone would say, "We are all adults and can do as we please." However, in the world of total responsibility, every decision you make plays into the results that happen in life. You are responsible for everything good or bad because of the decisions you make.

Let's go back to the person drinking now having to get up and be ready for this 8 a.m. meeting from a Total Responsibility standpoint and ask the following questions:

Did this person really make every decision in a flawless manner which resulted in not being ready for this meeting with a key client?

Should this person really have been drinking heavily at a bar?

Should this person really have been staying out late at night under these conditions?

In every situation in life there is usually something that a person can do to improve in terms of decision-making and how they could have made better choices. In the example of the person at the bar late at night, clearly there were areas of possible improvement.

Total Responsibility is born by the realization that everything in life you do ultimately plays a part in how it unfolds, either directly or indirectly. I would say this is a powerful moment because after realizing this I started thinking:

"Everything in my life is on my own burden to take care of and not the responsibility of anyone else other than myself. If I am responsible for everything in my life, then I might as well take complete control and ownership of all aspects of it anyway."

Here is my recommendation as you work to learn Total Responsibility. Answer these questions each time you find yourself wanting to blame others or circumstances for your outcomes:

What can I learn from this situation?

How can I get better moving forward after this lesson?

Did I really make every decision as best as I could?

How do my decisions impact my future?

How do my decisions impact others?

Most people in life have a victim mentality and blame others for all the things that happen to them. When you approach your purpose from any other perspective other than Total Responsibility, you have basically given your power to other people. Assigning your future to others means you can never really have any chance to reinvent yourself into the person you want to be.

After completing these three steps, you will have made a lot of progress that will be key to moving forward in your inner leadership development.

Now is the time to gather up some lions to come along with you on your journey and build your own lion pride.

Application Example: Liz's Purpose Branding & Embodiment

After I had completed building the Lion Attitude system in 2020, I was excited when I realized that I had built something special. But was this only a personal development process for a technical AEC professional like me or would it work on other people?

I was working at the government in the rough patch when I shared with a HVAC controls contractor my process of leadership development. There was something inside me that was saying I could help other people with this system I created.

But how would someone even consider working with me on some experimental system?

The contractor mentioned his daughter was struggling after college trying to find a job in the AEC industry. He felt it was a lack of purpose, one he had seen in me before my change.

With his permission, I reached out to Liz and started to get to know her better. Something inside me kept saying teaching her this system would have an IMPACT on her inner leadership issues. Liz told me something which was a pivotal moment of our relationship:

She wanted to use this system to get her first job in the workforce.

Liz was building inner leadership going through the process of Chapter One and Two with the Reinvention & Purpose Development. You could see her intention and motivation pushing her forward, but a key point was coming to a head.

What was the Purpose Statement that would be the reason she would keep moving forward?

Liz started the process just like me in Chapter Two, listening to motivational speeches on many of the websites I recommended. She heard speeches like Fearless Motivation and Fearless Soul. Liz chose a quiet place on the beach, since she lived in a town nearby.

She was working in a retail job back then, so her hours were inconsistent, varying between days and nights. But during those off hours, her sole focus was the development of her purpose. After some of our sessions, she would tell me about looking out on the water, staring at the ocean, trying to understand what she wanted her future to look like. It was a calming feeling she had never felt before after going there many times in the past.

Something was different about these trips now. Liz was putting on her headphones and listening to speeches while looking into the waves. She had all these questions listed in Chapter Three written down. Thinking deeply about the questions while the words of the speeches were going into her ears led her to a moment of clarity when the following words came out of her mouth:

"Hard Work Beats Talent"

Liz told me she was in tears when those words came out of her mouth. She was a hard-working student her entire life, making the right decisions. But the struggle to find a job made her wonder if this was going to be enough for the next step. Liz lost her purpose, and her inner leadership was weakened. She was losing the ability to see what amazing future could be out there for her. Liz had to be intentional and motivated to find it.

After this moment, Liz made a special necklace and wrote those words down so she could see them every day. She would say, "Hard work beats talent" to herself in the mirror each morning when she woke up. She shared with me that her purpose was now carried with her everywhere to remind her of who she wanted to be in this journey.

In the final step she started focusing on the Total Responsibility angle, looking at every single decision she was making in her job search.

Did Liz have the right strategy to get the job she wanted?

Was she interacting and building relationships with the right people?

Could Liz communicate her purpose and how she would IMPACT others seeking a role in the field of her choice?

What was Liz learning from the process and failures up to this point?

Liz had taken total control at this point of every single aspect of her purpose. I could feel the energy difference flowing in her, and honestly, to me as well. Her father called me about a month into the process and said:

"Kirby, I don't know what you said to Liz, but she is a completely different person. I have a feeling she is going to land a job pretty soon with this system you are teaching."

Fast forward about a month later into Liz's work with The Lion Attitude process and I get a call.

"Kirby, I got my very first job offer and it's exactly in the field that I wanted to work in. I am going to accept this and start work in the coming weeks!"

This was a moment of application of Phase One I will never forget. It was the first time I could see that what I had built would also work on others.

It's amazing the power of writing something down and how it develops purpose.

Chapter 4

Lion Pride Development

Your purpose is strong now. I commend you for putting in all this work to get to this point.

How does your energy level feel at this moment?

This stage of the purpose development is when you start to really notice the people around you and how much you have changed. You start to hear from others about how you have changed or grown going through this Phase One process.

When I think back to getting these comments from people around me, I honestly started laughing in my head thinking:

> **My goal was to develop my leadership skills and build them by developing my purpose from within. The objective of this was to reinvent myself and never go back. So yes, I have changed, and it looks like I am on my way.**

You might notice that the circle of people around looks a lot different now than when you started in Phase One. You might have stronger relationships with some in the circle while others might have faded into the background or disappeared completely. This is a key moment since your next steps are to start to carefully evaluate your circle and make the choices for how to develop your new lion pride. This will be part of your growth journey for the rest of the Phases in Two through Four.

Lions in the wild operate in a strong social culture called prides. Prides work together and push each other to grow and become stronger as a team. This statement, which I make often, is a relevant part of this step in the journey:

Lions only hang around other lions.

Lions want to be around animals that make them better and push them to levels they could not do alone. You will notice your leadership development gets stronger being around people who demonstrate the qualities needed to benefit our future. Here are some questions that are part of the discovery process around deciding who should be coming along for this journey with you:

Where should I start looking for people with leadership qualities that represent what I want to become as a leader?

Does being around this person make me feel like my leadership development is getting stronger or weaker?

Does this person support me in the direction I want to travel now and going forward in the rest of the steps outlined in this book?

What will I do when someone I think aligns with my mission doesn't as I make changes in my life?

In the next steps we will delve into all the concepts of finding your lion pride so you can find people who will raise your standards.

Step One – Evaluation of Your Surroundings

Charlie Tremendous Jones provided an eye-opening moment for me. He says the person you will be in the next five years is based on the books you read and the people you hang out with.

He gets into the concept that everything you choose to surround yourself with affects your life. All the thoughts, decisions, actions, anything you do in the present, will affect and shape the future life you are going to have.

The first time I heard the speech *Feed Your Mind* on Fearless Motivation, it references this quote from Charlie Tremendous Jones. It was powerful. I started to really look at many of the things in my life that were part of this old self I was trying to leave behind so my new reinvented self could fight toward the surface.

When I was a young kid, I remember my mom and dad always saying the company you keep reflects who you are. At the time I really didn't understand this very well, but Charlie Tremendous Jones had me looking back to all these situations.

I remember in high school spending time with people who were doing questionable things. The future I was thinking I wanted back then was very different than what I see today. After hearing this speech, I went into a very reflective evaluation of many aspects of my life and began to connect the dots of why I ended up in the positions I did back then.

I started asking myself these exercise questions, looking back on nearly every situation to see if I was making decisions that aligned with my future:

How did being around this person benefit my future?

How did making this decision benefit my future?

Are the people around me today aligned with the future that I want?

What skills can I learn, or what different actions do I need to take, to grow toward the future I want?

It was an interesting exercise. I could see that many of the low points were created by not having the right mindset, purpose, people, or tools in my life that encouraged the future I wanted. And for the first time in my life I realized, in a powerful moment, that I was responsible for everything that got me to this point. This included all the positive and negative outcomes. But at the same time, I realized I had control to make everything in the future the way I wanted it to be.

I use this analogy often in presentations. Let's say a person walks into a room of people who all have COVID. If a person that walks into this room doesn't have the virus and spends time around people who are infected, what do you think is going to eventually happen? I know this sounds like a major surprise, but ultimately an uninfected person will get the virus and become infected because of all the people he is spending his time with.

Every aspect of what you do today affects your future…even reading this book. And I hope reading this book affects your future in a positive way!

Step Two – Lion Pride Development

Lions have been revered in history for thousands of years by humankind, but very few people put in the work that lions do to allow them to be masters of their domain as an apex predator. This step focuses on how you can find people who align with the future you want to have.

So here are some of the questions I would recommend answering so you can find people who align with your future:

Where can I find people who align with my purpose?

What skills do I need to learn to attract people into my life?

What places do these people go to have lunch or professionally network?

I use the example of someone who wants to develop strong leadership skills as an architect in my field as part of their purpose. If I was this person, I would be spending as much time as possible learning all I can from successful architects in any professional organizational setting. If you want to be successful in life, you need to spend time with successful people.

Once again, lions only hang around other lions for a reason.

And the only time you will ever see a lion around any other animal is for this simple reason…it's the target!!!!

Step Three – Continuous Evaluations of your Lion Pride

You have worked hard and carefully chosen your new lion pride, which is going to be part of your path for leadership development. You've asked lots of questions and put in time focused on seeing who aligns with your new purpose. Now that you've asked the right questions, it seems like you can just put this on autopilot for the rest of this journey.

This sounds great in theory, but there is a small problem in the application of this in the real world. I am getting ready to drop a big surprise. YOU ARE NOT DONE!

How many people can count on friends they had in high school to be still around in your life now on a consistent, impactful basis?

As you would expect, there are changes that happen all the time in life. People change just as much as well. Picking out and finding people in your circle early on is important for getting started on the path for Phase One of the leadership development path toward unbreakable purpose. However, you also must always pay attention to your pride, since you are undergoing a transformation that depends on them as part of the journey to developing leadership skills.

To ensure your chosen pride contains the right people to help you continue to develop, do a deep evaluation once a year. Look at yourself and how you feel about the people around you now. Ask yourself these questions during this annual evaluation process:

How do I feel being around this person in my life?

Is being around this person helping me achieve my goals?

What do I think would happen if a person was not in my life anymore?

In this part of Phase One, I ran into a situation where I was put into a professional ethical dilemma based on my observations of an approach that was happening on some projects by higher level people. There was someone I was working with whom I felt was a "mentor" yet was not directly involved in the project but had a hand in leadership decisions in the organization. At that time, I felt like they were in my circle and valued their input while working with me on my leadership aims.

I remember seeing this situation unfold and knowing immediately some things were happening that I can say, looking back, didn't align with my purpose. And I remember that immediate feeling after sending numerous text messages and having conversations with this "mentor" regarding the ethical concerns I had around decisions made by upper leadership on the project in question.

What I discovered was that not only was this person not in my corner, but we never aligned on core values at all. It was one of the most disappointing moments that left me feeling like I was on an island alone in a really bad situation. It was at that moment this person needed to leave my lion pride immediately. I needed to minimize my contact with him to the lowest level possible.

Remember the room full of people with COVID?

My story behind this is an example that things will change as you do, so you always need to pay attention to everything around you to make sure it aligns with your purpose.

Step Four – Lions tread their own path if needed.

This is the most difficult part and is an indirect byproduct of Step Three when evaluating people who could potentially be part of your lion pride. This is going to be one of the hardest moments in testing how strong your purpose is in your leadership development.

You also may be tasked with making the decision to walk away from everything and everyone if nothing around you aligns with the purpose you have found during this part of the process.

> **Yes, I really mean my recommendation is to walk away from everything and everyone if you need to and go on your own journey alone. But keep in mind this is a temporary part of the journey and not a permanent thing.**

Walking alone is one of the hardest things in life. We as humans need connection to survive just like lions in the wild need their pride.

I knew I would need to eliminate a lot of things in my life and walk alone for some period during Phase One of the reinvention and purpose development transformation. In my specific case, I had to clean up nearly everything in my old circle since I discovered none of it aligned with the type of leader I wanted to be. In the first year of all this journey described in the book, I was on an island alone with very little support for most of my time.

The thought of doing anything alone would have scared me to death earlier in my life. For many years I always wanted to fit in to be like all the others. The person I became in Step Three required developing methods to ensure I had a strong lion pride around me.

I was undergoing a transformation of every aspect of who I was down to the very core to build my leadership skills from nothing. I had never done all the items mentioned in Phase One before. There was no way I was going to be going back to my old self as a professional.

What I started to notice during this reinvention and my purpose development was a pivotal moment that showed how willing I was to put in the work to develop my leadership from within. And in the end, I started to attract people with the lion qualities I wanted into my life.

**New people entered my life aligned
with my purpose.
I was not alone anymore!**

During this part of the development of my leadership and purpose, my wife was not sure what was happening to me or what I was building from within. I was learning to harness the lion's power and channel it based on the Intention + Motivation concept of building purpose. This purpose and reinvention in Phase One would allow me to stay focused on my goals during even the worst of times.

The lion has now been awakened and it's in a very raw form right now, but the next leg of the journey is where you can really harness the lion's power of purpose.

After all, you are not alone anymore. I will be walking with you into Phase Two to develop an intentional start-up routine focused on self-development in the mornings. With Phase One and Two implemented together, your newly built purpose will become unbreakably strong on your journey to build better inner leadership as an AEC professional.

Application Example: Zach's Lion Pride Development

When I was employed in the government job, there was someone special who I started working with named Zach. Zach was a great individual contributor as an electrician and was taking a job in our department to be a supervisor for the first time. I got to interview him as part of a team and knew there was something special about him.

Zach had purpose. There was no doubt on the direction he wanted to travel in life. The people reporting to him enjoyed his ability to connect with them and troubleshoot issues from all his years of technical expertise. He was well liked in nearly every level of the organization.

Then something came along that no one saw coming . . .

An unexpected change in leadership took place and now he was reporting to a new person who didn't have a technical background or understand him as an AEC professional.

On the surface it seemed like everything was going decent with this new leader. However, deep down, Zach felt like something was off about the situation. In his day-to-day activities, he was surrounded by people who had similar technical mindsets, including me. This part of his job was still going great, but the leadership people he was working with started to fall out of alignment. Management above him was asking him to perform tasks that he knew would not be effective from a technical standpoint.

I remember him coming to me, telling me about some of the decisions management was making. It was clear to me Zach was frustrated with the outcomes. It turned out he was right that those decisions didn't have a chance to be successful from a technical perspective. Zach shared with me something that really stood out and reminded me of my own journey in Chapter Four.

"Kirby, these people above me don't align with where I want to go."

I could feel Zach's energy levels around intention and motivation draining with each day that he continued working with this new leadership group. It's not a surprise, looking at Zach's purpose, to see his strength was weakening over time. But Zach was different. He knew changes needed to be made.

Zach started paying attention to everyone around him in every aspect of their interactions with him plus listening to his own inner leadership built on purpose. Who made him feel good about the direction he wanted to go? Who was an energy drainer who was not good for his future? How could he spend more time around people he wanted to help him grow?

You can see, looking at this application, Zach was evaluating his lion pride. He needed to know who should be in and who needed to go to keep his purpose strong.

This sent Zach on a journey to reach out to other electrician friends he had worked with at his previous job. He started delving further into what specifically made him unhappy about the new leadership. Zach was trying to understand every aspect about why he felt the way he did around people who made him feel good (or not).

In the short term, this really helped Zach minimize his time around energy drainers and focus on people who could benefit his future. He started attending professional organizations in the electrical field, meeting some amazing people who would become part of his new lion pride. About six months later, he gave me a call to tell me something I will never forget.

"Kirby, I am going back to my old employer, taking a new position as a head of the electrical department. All the time I spent building my lion pride led me to find out my old supervisor was retiring in the future. The supervisor found out I was investing in myself. The first person he recommended for his replacement was me."

Zach's effort to build a new lion pride based on inner leadership with purpose was the reason he got this job. He also knew that the new leadership at his current job were not good for his future. As a result, it was time to make some changes and seek new opportunities.

This application of how to develop a lion pride is a great example of the statement below:

Lions only spend time with other lions.

Phase 2

Inner Leadership –
The Morning Start Up

We have made it through the first leg of the system called the Lion Attitude and put the infrastructure in place to start on a long journey together. The next component of the journey toward rebuilding your inner leadership development is to create intentional daily habits and keep the motivation going at the micro-level. Focusing on the small habits outlined in the Morning Start Up each day with Intention + Motivation will allow you to advance your purpose built in Phase One.

Self-development is a critical component to enhance your leadership development as an AEC professional. When I think of self-development, the first thing that comes into my head is football. One of the most interesting and enjoyable moments for me is watching the NFL Draft, and specifically the 1st round on Thursday night. There are all these NFL hopefuls wondering how their entire life's worth of work will play out. All the action happens behind the scenes with the general managers of the thirty-two teams in the league. Teams will make trades up and down in the draft, going after the players they want to help build their roster for the next season. Selection hopes are set on making the right decisions to lead them to the ultimate prize: winning the Super Bowl ring.

Successful people who are drafted tell their stories afterwards of all the hard work, the weight sessions, brutal practices, sacrifices made on the field, focusing on nutrition, working with coaches on their mental game, and getting the right team in place to put themselves in the best position for their upcoming professional career. One of the most heart-warming moments is seeing the 1st round picks hugging their family and significant others in the green room after their cell phone rings to hear a team calling to say, "We are excited to have you on the Carolina Panthers, are you ready to work?" The draft pick then walks on the stage with their hat and jersey with their number on it, then usually gives the NFL Commissioner, Roger Goodell, a big hug or a handshake.

All these players who are drafted have been intentionally working on their craft, motivated to get into the NFL with nothing swaying them from their objective. Based on the formula Intention + Motivation = Purpose, it makes sense most who follow this system daily have a chance to make it to the NFL.

But as we know in life, there's a big difference between getting drafted and making an impact in the NFL. We see stories of players like Ryan Leaf and Jamarcus Russell who excelled in college doing all the right things up to this point. And then it all falls apart as they fail to adapt to all the daily aspects of playing in the league, the offseason work, film sessions, and handling things off the field like a professional. Many of these items are not in a playbook they can simply read but a product of doing the small things daily at an intentional level. This can ultimately lead to the big results.

Players who end up being a bust in the league usually don't focus on the important things anymore. NFL league reporters ask questions like, "Ryan Leaf had it all. Why did it not work out for him?" Ultimately, the reason players who are successful make it is because they focus on specific areas each day, no matter what is going on in their life. And these components are some of the same things that AEC professionals do as well. Here is the big surprise secret of most successful people:

Successful leaders have a solid morning routine focused on self-development before they start their day!

Since I am in the AEC community, the first thing I thought of was an expensive piece of HVAC equipment I see daily. All manufacturers have specific instructions on how equipment must be started up correctly to operate properly. There are many checks and steps that take place before you finally flip the switch and turn on HVAC equipment. This ensures everything is done right so the equipment will last for a long time.

HVAC equipment also gets frequent routine maintenance to make sure that everything keeps running right during the duration of its useful life. And when we don't take care of our HVAC equipment in the construction and maintenance world, then the life of the parts is usually reduced. This can lead to large, expensive failures of components down the road. There is a phrase that I always hear about cars when people buy them. That's why we hear stories about how some car has the original engine after 300,000 miles on it that show this phrase to be true: *"If you take care of your car, it will take care of you."*

Starting up your day is just like starting up a piece of very expensive HVAC equipment. Or taking care of a car. If you follow the right daily steps and procedures, focused on helping you become your best self, then your day will go right as well. Taking care of yourself daily is a key component of being your best self, which is a function of strengthening your purpose in leadership development. This makes you best equipped to go after your mission and purpose that we covered, and you hopefully discovered, in Phase One.

These six steps will be outlined in detail during the subsequent sections of Phase Two:

Reading

Meditation

Gratitude

Exercise & Nutrition

Journaling & Reflection

5AM Club

The origins of all six of these components in the Morning Start Up are based on information I was listening to after I discovered my purpose and was working to strengthen it. I started to notice that these are the common practices that successful people prioritize and integrate into their lives as their morning routine.

On a Sunday afternoon I was listening to speeches on my favorite sites Fearless Motivation and Fearless Soul. As I listened to a lot of this material over time, I realized something my engineering logic started to put together:

"Kirby, if all these successful people have a strong morning routine and have these practices in common, then clearly I need to start adding these to my game plan as part of my purpose, right?"

What I learned by integrating these six components into my mission and purpose daily was that my level of intention hit new levels. Each of these areas allowed me to keep operating like a well-maintained piece of HVAC equipment. Properly maintained people and HVAC equipment have something in common: they can last a very long time doing a great job when they're well taken care of!

Chapter 5

Reading

There have been countless articles and information circulated around for many years that talk about how reading things makes you a better person. When we are in school, there are things like book clubs with an emphasis on reading all the way through college. Reading was a necessary evil for me back then, since I needed to do it as part of getting through school. But to be honest, I hated reading and enjoyed all the science/math topics in school a lot more. I guess that was how I became attracted to engineering in the beginning.

Soft skills were something that never really made a lot of sense to me. This was the case even once I started focusing on being more social after I got my engineering license in 2013. I remember my old boss back then. He started to teach me some of the basics and was constantly referencing books or material he was using to expand his mind. One of the books that he mentioned was called *The Platinum Rule* by Dr. Tony Alessandra and Michael O'Connor.

The book was a simplified version of the DISC chart, putting the four personalities into categories of Director, Socializer, Relator, and Thinker. This book provided the origins of my journey back into reading. For the first time ever in my life, there was a clear purpose behind how reading would impact my life. I started to figure out that reading books like this in areas I wanted to grow in would result in me having a better future.

I was a bare minimum reader with no enthusiasm about reading. I had to work hard at establishing a habit for something that I had avoided for almost my entire adult life. Of course, I started to pick out books that aligned with my new mission and purpose. And I started to realize how significant of an opportunity I missed by not reading as I started my journey into self-development.

As my journey began, I read for about thirty minutes a day, either during a lunch break or in the evening before bed. I noticed that the more I put time into reading, the more enlightened I felt overall. Many of the books I consumed were focused on leadership, business, and soft skills. Each one made me stronger and caused me to level up more.

For the first time ever in my life, reading became something that I was excited to do. I wanted to learn more things to benefit my future! Many of the books I read have influenced my ability to get better daily.

Step One – Rome wasn't Built in a Day

You might be a person just like me who didn't like reading at all, or you might be doing this already in your life. If you are reading already, this step will be a lot easier than it was for me.

The goal of reading is to put more intentional daily focus on feeding your mind with successful and positive things. Reading this book right now is hopefully part of your experience that you can check off as benefiting your future with a positive impact.

For the people who don't like to read, you might have an issue with attention span. It can feel like drudgery if you're trying to force yourself too fast into a habit that you have never done before or even cared about. Start slow and pace yourself by simply breaking down the thirty minutes into smaller parts, if half an hour seems like too much. Even if you need to start with five-minute increments, or a specific small number of pages a day, that's effort and an accomplishment that should make you proud. Les Brown says reading anything, even a simple ten to fifteen pages of positive material, will have an impact on making you better than you were before.

Over time, you will find yourself building momentum. I promise you, the reading will become easier. For some, the reading sessions might fit better in the evening before bed (aka bedtime reading). I found the best fit for me was reading, if possible, before starting what used to be the beginning of my day. In the final part of the Morning Start Up, I will share more about what I did to help me add this into my day. As a result, I was able to start my workday with extra zip and energy that I didn't have before.

Step Two – Book Selections

So, you are ready to start reading and in the right mindset to add these magical thirty minutes into your life to be a better person, right? There are millions of books that you can pick. Anything you can read that will be positive material is a good start.

There is only one very simple rule you need to keep in mind when focusing on reading:

The thirty minutes a day of reading must benefit your purpose plus help grow your inner leadership!

You can choose to read all kinds of things in life and on social media. Some things will make you better, while many things will have no impact on your future purpose.

The goal behind this section is reading things that, at the end of the reading session, will result in growth and expansion of your mind for your inner leadership development. A great strategy is focusing on areas where you want to grow your leadership skills.

Below are some general self-development reading ideas to help you start finding books to read as part of your thirty-minute routine:

Communication
Understanding Personality Types
Emotional Intelligence
Public Speaking
Team Building
Presentation Strategy
Technical Skill Books
Time Management
Goal Setting
Change Management
Relationship Building

Below is a sample list of books I've read which had a big impact on me. You may want to consider picking up one or more of the following:

Emotional Intelligence 2.0, Travis Bradberry & Jean Graves
Leadership 2.0, Travis Bradberry & Jean Graves
Think and Grow Rich, Napoleon Hill
Pink Goldfish, Stan Phelps and David J. Rendall
No Fail Communication, Michael Hyatt
The Platinum Rule, Tony Alessandra

Bonus Strategy: Studying for professional licenses, educational classes, or certifications that could enhance your future completely count as part of your daily thirty minutes. An example of this was when I spent thirty minutes a day for a few months working on my Certified Energy Auditor Exam (by Association of Energy Engineers) preparation.

Clearly, this material benefited my future, helped me develop inner leadership skills, and allowed my income to rise, so there was a return on investment for the time put into this. I was not reading books at the time I did any certification preparation since I was learning something new, investing time in my education.

Application Example: Kirby's Struggles with Reading

It's easy to sit here and tell you about the thirty minutes of reading. However, I wanted to share an example of the application of my own reading to help you, the reader, understand it's a process developed over time.

There was a Les Brown speech called "Face Your Fears," where he talked about reading ten to fifteen pages of material every day that would benefit your future. When I got to this step, I started thinking about what material I wanted to read.

Was there an interesting book out there that would help my skills grow?

In the beginning of this step, I was specific about picking books that were interesting to me, where I could see the value of what I was reading. By doing this, it was easier for me to get those ten to fifteen pages in, building up my commitment over time. For parts of the book where I was struggling, I would even try to read the material more than once so I could better absorb what was being taught.

Over time, my reading ability got a lot better. It also became easier to dig into material that I wasn't directly interested in. The next question helped me get over the hump after building the momentum above.

"What books and material can you read that will allow you to make more income or create more I+M+P+A+C=T?"

When you think about reading material with this perspective, it's easier to pursue your purpose. After reflecting on increasing my IMPACT, I could even read very dry material, since I knew there it would benefit my future in the long run. If I ran into a setback, then I went back to the basics of the ten to fifteen pages of material, until I got back to thirty minutes of reading again.

Now it's time to journey into the next step of the Morning Start Up.

Chapter 6

Meditation

When I first heard the speech about meditation having an impact on your day, I honestly started laughing because I didn't believe this could work. I had this image in my head about some monk in the middle of a temple in a pose chanting and making noises for hours on end. I am a pretty on-the-go type of person. I had my newfound purpose but was still refining the process of how to use this effectively during my daily life.

My logic started to shift when I researched the benefits of meditation. There is significant scientific evidence that shows meditation provides the following benefits when you integrate it into your daily practice:

- Stress reduction
- Stronger Self-Awareness (key component of emotional intelligence)
- Reduced Negative Self Talk or Thoughts
- Improved Memory
- Improved Overall Physical Health
- Better Sleep Patterns

Little did I know then the impact meditation was to have on my life, especially in situations of high stress. I was shifting my mindset into being both a designer and the team project manager at the same time. This was also the first phase of my life change beginning in 2013, where I started to learn soft skills from scratch.

When you are a designer at an engineering firm, there are lots of quiet days sitting at your desk drafting and designing systems for buildings. Most of your time is spent utilizing many software tools or calculation programs. In some cases, you could go a couple of days without possibly speaking to a person at all. Communication happens mostly via email internally to teammates or externally to a client. My shift into being a more external facing person was very hard with no leadership training. I stressed out a lot, worrying about how I was going to learn how to communicate with people and lead internal teams.

I was also concerned about being completely responsible for my work as a professional engineer. This was a major mind shift that I thought I was prepared for. The reality was that nothing could have truly prepared me for this transition.

After I started working on a project as a newly licensed professional engineer, I was assigned a specific BBQ restaurant job to put my newly earned seal on as the designer of record for the first time. It was a very high-profile project that was near the American Tobacco Historic District in Durham, NC.

There was a major issue with the kitchen hood design I was battling back and forth. I couldn't get clear on how to resolve it. During those times, and many others when I was stressed out, I would notice that my body would wake me up around 3 a.m. Back then I would try to do all kinds of things to go back to sleep. Usually nothing would work. I would try sitting out on the couch to avoid waking up my wife. In many cases, I would simply be up for the day. As you would expect, that day was usually a sluggish one, which resulted in me having low energy levels and being a shell of myself.

My first thoughts turned to the impact on my sleep patterns, but I had other reasons for considering meditation. You can guess by the questions below I looked at this like it's an engineering task that I completed, just like anything else during my professional career.

What was I supposed to be thinking about during a meditation session?
Is there a proper way to meditate?
Should I meditate in the morning or evening?
How long should I meditate during a session?
What happens if I can't control my thoughts when I meditate?
Should I sit on the couch or lay down when I do this?
How long does it take to see an impact from meditation?

As I started meditating in early 2020, it was hard to disconnect all the rapid thoughts in my head or concerns about doing it correctly. Something the meditation trainer said during the session stuck with me. It's the idea that the thoughts are just something you watch from a third person perspective. You will see the thought and acknowledge it, but the key is to be able to just keep moving on after recognizing it.

Over time, after fighting through many sessions daily for months, I started to see the impact of all the benefits of meditation. The one that I was the most focused on was ending those unwelcome sleep interruptions in the middle of the night. I also wanted to achieve more sustainable management of my overall stress levels. At the time, my logic was if I did a session right before bed to let my mind reset, it would help me have a better night's sleep.

The main reason why I recommend this, and decided to add this step to my life, is because it ended nearly all my racing mind moments and the stress that was waking me up at 3 a.m. If I did manage to still wake up on a rare occasion, then I completed meditation sessions on the couch in the middle of the night to calm my racing mind. It's been a long time since I've had one of those 3 a.m. moments, but this is just a small example of the impact meditation has had on my life.

It's also interesting to see how my self-awareness improved because of meditation. I knew the second I woke up at 3 a.m. the exact reasons why. From that moment of awareness, I could then take action to take control of my mind and not let it be the reason poor sleep impacted me the next day. I didn't envision myself adding this to my routine back then. But as I mentioned before, if successful people in life were doing this, then clearly it had value. I decided to add it to my routine as well.

Let's walk through the steps to getting mindfulness integrated into your mornings so you can develop tools to have stronger leadership.

Step One – Meditation Tools

There are many different options to look at in the meditation space, including the website (and phone app) *Calm* and *Headspace*. There are also many different free YouTube videos to follow along as you start your journey into this realm. You can choose to have some soothing music as part of your meditation session or do a more traditional guided meditation with a speaker if that helps.

My favorite session is something called the *Daily Calm* by Tamara Levitt. The session is usually ten to twelve minutes long. There are often some positive learning moments that she describes during the session near the end. It's interesting hearing her stories daily. In one session she described going to a retreat to sit for six to eight hours for a single session. This is honestly incredible when you think about me simply recommending a basic ten- to twelve-minute session once a day. She does this for nearly an entire workday.

The *Calm* app on my phone tracks my activity and consistency. The longest chain of days was 176 days straight, so far, anyway. At the end of each session, I always feel clearer headed and ready to tackle the other aspects of the Morning Start Up.

One of the things I noticed over time was how not doing meditation affected my performance. I noticed its impact on my leadership from an emotional intelligence perspective, sleep quality, or mental focus. I started to eventually not beat myself up over breaking a streak by missing a session, and simply moved on to the next day like nothing ever happened.

The major point of adding this is that rather than attaining perfection, you're using the Morning Start Up to have a greater impact on your day in your quest to strengthen your purpose.

Step Two – Setup for your Meditation Sessions

For my mindfulness sessions, I was originally focused on the nighttime session to make it so I could go to sleep without waking up. Once that was resolved, I switched to meditating in the morning when I woke up. My meditation routine involves getting settled on the couch or laying down on the floor in my carpeted office. If I am laying on the floor, I spread my arms and legs out so I can stretch my body out as much as possible. If I am sitting, I gently rest my hands on my stomach.

There is a big focus on breathing during the sessions, which helps me build a good rhythm in the first one to two minutes. It's surprising how simply breathing mindfully helps eliminate tension.

In Step One, I described the tools to use, but I'll cover the lengths of the session more deeply here. Experts recommend ten to twenty minutes a day, so for me, doing the *Daily Calm* session is easy, since I know after that is over, I have completed this amount of time. You might find yourself doing both a morning and evening session if you have a very stressful day. I would recommend doing the evening session within thirty minutes of going to bed. Think of this time as what I call a "meditation flush out" to wipe away all the things in your head and allow for a full night of quality rest.

There have been some occasions when I fell asleep during the session since I was in such a deep state. Don't be surprised if this happens to you as well, particularly if you are doing this in the evening. For morning sessions, it seems to help get you out of that half asleep state that occurs right after you get out of bed. By the end of the morning session, I am wide awake and full of energy, ready to work on all the Morning Start Up steps.

While this is what works for me and was part of my journey to develop inner leadership skills, there are many ways to meditate. Do what works best for you. The most important thing behind the sessions is doing the work to become the best version of yourself to support your purpose as a leader daily. No one is giving you a grade on it. You aren't going to be fired from your job if things don't go perfectly.

Application Example: Connie's Meditation Place

I met Connie during my travels around the country as part of my role at work. We had seen each other at a conference a while back. Since I was traveling to her home area, it made perfect sense to connect with her while I was there.

Connie was curious about this book and what I was writing about the Morning Start Up part and, specifically, the topic of meditation. She shared her stress was high in the work she does in the energy sector of the AEC industry. Over time, she could feel her self-management also becoming weakened. Something needed to change.

She first found a place in her house that would be her safety area to meditate. Interestingly enough, it was an area of her closet. Connie set up a nice pillow she could sit on and created a space where she could go when things got stressful. Each session she would access her meditation app on her phone and settle in on the cushion. The first sessions were hard. She was wondering what success was supposed to look like. Negative self-doubt creeped in as she questioned the value of doing this practice.

Her focus eventually led her to simply working on the breath. Something that came up as she described her sessions was thinking she could control her thoughts. The voice on the meditation app suggested thinking of those thoughts like clouds rolling by on a sunny day. You see the clouds and recognize what they are but try not to be swept away by the sight of them.

Over the course of the next few months, Connie was doing this every morning at wake-up time and in the evening before bed. She described the feeling of how freeing it was having a clear head during the day. If there was a super stressful situation at work, Connie found herself going to that area of her closet to do an "emergency session" to try and reset, keeping herself from getting carried away by the intensity of the moment.

This was a powerful reinforcement of my own journey through meditation and why it's part of the Morning Start Up. Now we are on to the next piece of the puzzle to add to your routine, gratitude.

Chapter 7

Gratitude

As I started to read about this concept, there was a big internal battle in my head. My newfound purpose was a game changer for me, and it was getting stronger as I went through these steps. I really started digging back far into my past to figure out if I was focusing on gratitude at all during my life.

In my logical head, I was thinking that I had parents who loved me and raised me the best they could growing up in the small town of Kinston, NC. My father was an HVAC contractor and a 2nd generation business owner, taking over from my grandfather, who started the construction company in the 50s. My mother stayed at home for the earliest days that I could remember and worked with my dad as my sister and I grew up into our teenage years.

We went on lots of trips together. Looking at us from the outside in, we had all the things of an upper middle-class upbringing that should have built a strong foundation for my success later in life. Both my sister and I went to private school. We had access to a car at age sixteen, right off the bat. My parents paid for and put me through college. For the most part, I had access to nearly anything I wanted. I was able to secure a job in engineering with the ideas my dad had suggested based on my interest in HVAC.

One would think I would have been on this cruise course to a comfortable life with all the things you could have ever asked for. Yet somehow, I was sitting in a car in Cary, NC, realizing I was unhappy, unfulfilled, and stressed.

How was it possible for me to have all these advantages that many kids likely didn't have, only for me to be sitting here in this car feeling miserable as an adult at age forty-two?

As I started to really dive deep into the concept of gratitude building as part of the Morning Start Up, it hit me like a heavy brick. I went through life with little resistance, getting everything I wanted. Many of the issues I battled were self-created, due to my assumption that I could "outsmart the room" without putting any effort toward getting by in life. Or in many cases, it was always seeing if my parents or someone else could bail me out of a situation that I got into growing up.

I realized, looking back on all this, I had gone through nearly all my life not learning the basics of how to be grateful. No wonder I was lacking (or falling short) in my own leadership development abilities.

There was part of me that honestly felt ashamed that nearly my whole life was built without applying this simple concept. As I started to listen to speeches, strengthening my purpose, for the first time I was feeling the ability to learn gratitude. In my mind, I felt like I got a second chance in life to start over with my reinvention. I was going to make sure that I made the most of it.

I started to realize the profound impact of being grateful every day. A lot of questions came up as I integrated this into my practice. One of the things that I noticed was how different I felt as I replayed the negative situations in the years leading up to me feeling unhappy, unfulfilled, and stressed with no purpose. I will never forget these phrases, which impact my life, even today.

> # There is always something to be grateful for in life.
> # You can't be negative and genuinely grateful at the same time.

Gratitude and a positive mindset have health benefits that have been documented extensively. Below are some of the benefits that come from adding a gratitude practice to your day and why it's a start-up step in the morning routine.

- Reduce Depression
- Less Stress & Anxiety
- Better Heart Health
- Better Sleep at Night

It's amazing when you think about how powerful a positive and thankful mindset can impact your health.

Let's walk into the journey of adding this important part of the Morning Start Up into your day.

Step One – Always Find Something to be Grateful For

During the time I was integrating Morning Start Up into my life, I was forced to take on a construction manager role. This was against my wishes. I hated this job change and was miserable. The construction manager role was nothing remotely like the job I was interested in when I started working there. I was hired as a Mechanical Engineer who would be working as an owner's representative.

This government work was emotionally draining every day. After this change happened, I was feeling resentful about all the struggles of doing a role I had zero interest in. I didn't have a lot of support to succeed either; "management" above me didn't seem to care about my well-being or development. To add even more to the challenge, COVID came, and we were isolated, working remotely with limited peer support in my new department. From my perspective, this felt like a complete setup to fail in all aspects of the job.

I implemented the concept of gratitude, which is the reason I am even here sharing this experience. My first step was to make a phone call to people who had supported me in the past on my journey up to where I was at that moment. If it was too early in the morning, then I would send a text message or an email to someone to read.

In the early days of doing this, I am not sure how much impact gratitude had, since maybe people around me didn't take it seriously. I was simply calling to express how grateful I was for something they did for me and didn't expect anything in return. This was the first time in my life I had done anything like this. It honestly felt freeing being able to do this. Eventually, I started to see a major impact in myself and others around me.

Nearly every relationship changed for me over time with my family, my wife, and others in my professional world. Gratitude was a major component of it. During those dark times working for the government doing something I never wanted, I was starting to develop genuine authentic relationships with team members and peers simply because of expressing gratitude for anything a person did for me. The gratitude was the reason I was going to fight for my purpose daily.

It's now become so ingrained in my mind, you will hear me in almost any greeting speak to a person with gratitude:

"I am grateful to connect with you today."
"I am grateful that what I did brought value for you."

This is why I recommend, when you wake up, to express you're genuinely grateful to at least one person for something they did for you. If you keep doing this daily, expect your life to change for the better and your health as well. You can also write a handwritten note expressing gratitude or send an email at an unexpected time slot, so a person is surprised when they see it.

Over time you will see the impact. It won't take long to see how it brings life and energy to all the relationships around you. You will be a better leader with a grateful attitude. Your team will improve as well.

Step Two – Being Grateful Shuts Down Negative Mindsets

This idea around the powerful impact of gratitude on your overall well-being sounds good in theory. But is it possible for us to be grateful and positive all the time? I was listening to a speech where someone was asking this exact question. I'll never forget the speaker's response.

Question: How can I be always positive and grateful?
Answer: Not be human…

We can never be in a 100% perfect state of being grateful all the time. Negative situations are going to happen with no way to avoid them. But I would say that being able to shift your mind from a negative to a positive perspective is a learned skill that changes everything in the gratitude realm.

Taking the same situation I was describing above with the government will be a great example of how to reframe it in a positive way. Let's look at its uses in the Step Two part of Gratitude:

That dark time working for the government, with poor leadership around me, doing something I didn't want professionally, had me concentrating on my purpose daily with a razor-like focus. My goal was to find ways to improve myself during those times, no matter how bad things were for me. I knew I was going to have a better life afterwards by focusing on myself and staying positive as much as possible. I had a stable income and was not working a lot of hours, so I had the ability to work on developing other aspects of my life. My wife and family were supportive of my transformation. So were key people who could see all the effort I was putting in to reinvent myself.

One of the key people who I collaborated with many years ago ultimately led me to the opportunity I have now. I left the government job and now enjoy working in HVAC technical sales in the Southeast. The government work led me to create this specialized leadership development system with the goal of helping other AEC technical professionals find their purpose to build strong leadership skills. My goal behind The Lion Attitude is to offer a system so others don't have to struggle like I did as I found myself in an AEC leadership position.

Reflecting on the situation I went through, it doesn't sound as bad with all the growth and lessons learned that came from the struggle. That knowledge put me in a better position as a leader in all aspects so that I can grow even more today and beyond. With that said, I am not perfectly grateful in every single negative situation all the time.

But day by day, I hope to wear that negative voice down to a whimper.

As you work on the skill of having your mind quickly shift into a positive mindset over time, you will see the shift in this aspect of gratitude. And you will also see relationships with people around you change as your leadership skills improve. Try to look at a negative mindset from a positive viewpoint at least once a day and watch the magic happen.

Application Example: Kirby's Gratitude Calls & Text Messages

When I started thinking about gratitude while adding this focus to my daily practice, I pondered some of the questions below:

Can I really find something to be grateful for every day?

Would someone really think I was being genuine if I did this?

Could I feel better, having better inner leadership and self-management like described in the steps, making this effort?

I remember it started with using phone calls while I was exercising in the morning during the summer of 2019. One of the first people I contacted was the instructor who helped build my process of purpose development. We started to build a deeper connection. It's important to note that this must be genuine, heartfelt gratitude to create IMPACT. People will be able to spot fake gratitude a mile away.

Here's what I remember saying to my Covey instructor when I connected months later with gratitude on my mind:

"Lin, the Covey class you did was a life-changing moment for me. I took away something really special from it. For the first time, I understand my purpose and have been working on it daily. I am grateful for being able to meet you because of that class and wanted to share the impact you had on me due to your work."

Lin was completely surprised by this call. I remember how I felt from an energy standpoint. It gave me extra life during the day knowing I made a difference in someone else's. Over time, I started getting excited each day, thinking about someone who did something I could be grateful for and telling them about how much I appreciated them for it.

Sometimes this was a short phone call. Other times, it was a text message early in the morning. Here is an example text I sent to someone recently:

"Maggie, just wanted to let you know I was grateful for your support of me when I needed it. You had an impact on my day and on me."

Spreading positive messages and energy to people makes everyone feel better. This also builds strong inner leadership and self-management skills, putting focus on intention and motivation.

Chapter 8

Physical Health

When I was sitting in the car that day realizing my purpose, I was thinking about doing two things: losing weight and developing a great plan for my Triangle ASHRAE Chapter. I was to start my second term leading the team on July 1st. None of the things that ultimately happened or have been written about in this book were on my mind, but I knew something had to change so I could get to the places I wanted to head in life.

For years, I had battled weight and health issues. That's because of me, once again, assuming the "smarter than the room" mentality during childhood and college. For all my young life, I was a healthy weight and never gained, no matter how much I was eating daily. In my mind I was invincible, with no concern about what would start to happen as soon as college ended.

Of course, while in the early years and college, I was very active in all kinds of sports like basketball, running, and bowling. During college there was tons of walking around the NC State campus carrying a heavy backpack with course books and materials for classes. I was also involved in intramural bowling team stuff, which was a lot of fun.

Now, suddenly, I got my first professional job in Greenville, NC as an HVAC designer working for a start-up engineering company. Things were different. My eating didn't really change, but my activity levels started to drop significantly. I was staying behind a desk for hours on end learning programs like AUTOCAD and other software to develop my skills as a mechanical engineer in the MEP design world.

From 2001 to 2002, my weight started to go up. The same mentality and decision-making that was negatively affecting other areas of my life was putting me in a poor situation with my health. I gained fifty pounds. When I moved back to Raleigh for another engineering job, I realized I'd have to put in the work to maintain a healthy lifestyle. I started using Weight Watchers Online, since it was a mathematical system that an engineer could understand. Each food in the system is assigned points and you get points for activity levels.

Using an engineered system by Weight Watchers was how I lost weight back then. I was exercising daily with weights and cardio in my new apartment in Raleigh, plus eating Lean Cuisines to keep my points within reasonable levels. This is where my action focus, which will be covered in Phase Three, was a strength, since I just needed to follow a specific system and the work would get me to an outcome I wanted. Everything sounds perfect, right?

Unfortunately, this is where my old self came back, because I didn't have the core concepts I write about in this book developed in my life. After hitting my target weight for the first time, I stopped working out and wasn't focusing on myself daily. Fast forward to 2008 and I had gained all the weight back and even more.

I recommitted to losing weight in 2008, feeling certain there would be no way I would go back again for a second time to my old weight. My wife and I went on the journey to lose weight together. We went back to the Weight Watchers Online system that had been successful for me in the past. It took lots of walking and hard work to lose 100 pounds this time. I remember the day I hit my goal weight. I made a specific effort that day to leave work in the morning, since I forgot to weigh in earlier and knew I was close to my goal. When I got home, I discovered I hit my goal. I was so excited to see this mark!

Here is where my old self apparently didn't learn anything from 2002. The very first thing I did after getting to the goal was go right back to eating as I did while gaining weight. The 2008 weight goal was a big deal for me. I was going to use this as a springboard of confidence to attempt the Professional Engineering exam for the third time with a legitimate effort. That didn't happen when I had taken the test in 2005 and 2006. I remember talking with my boss back then about my exam plans after hitting my weight loss goal. He offered to quiz me about specific concepts as I started putting effort into this endeavor.

I remember one day struggling to answer questions my boss asked as part of my daily prep. I'll never forget what he said to me as I was still failing to grasp some of the concepts. It changed everything. I never forgot his words:

> **"Kirby, you might have put in all this work to lose weight, but you don't have what it takes to be a Professional Engineer."**

This was a moment that changed every aspect of my life. I completely lost all confidence in myself. Poor leadership caused by lack of positive support for my effort to improve myself played a direct role in this feeling. I became convinced this supervisor didn't care about my wellbeing and desire for growth.

Ultimately, in 2009, I left that engineering firm and was ready to give up on my goal of being a professional engineer. I ended up working for a sheet metal ductwork fabrication company for a short stint before coming back into engineering again with a different mindset. My weight ballooned, having put back on what I had already lost twice, including the 100 pounds since the last time. All the great things were starting to happen in 2013 for my career, but I was still not taking care of myself so I could live up to my complete potential.

There was a key component to both my weight loss and gains. I realized this looking back as I started a third journey to work on my health. How was I going to avoid going back for a third time and not suffer the see-saw effect I had experienced in the past? What was missing back then? How could I do this differently after listening to inspiring motivational speeches?

The key component I was missing was a strong purpose that would keep me going regardless of what others thought of me. I also needed to look at the root causes of why I ended up going back to old patterns after the previous two attempts. As I sat in the house, by myself, reciting my purpose (**Courage, Strength, Bravery, Leadership, & Heart**) in the mirror, something was different this time. I decided to never go back to the person I was looking at during that moment. I was going to make this happen regardless of anything or anyone's opinions or thoughts behind what I was doing.

I knew at that moment that taking care of my body and health was an important thing now, which would be the reason I could do lots of things I wanted to in the future. I had a strong purpose to focus on myself in a way I had never felt before. I needed to be a great purpose-based leader for myself first, so that I could use my focus to serve and support others later.

Let's walk through my journey in 2019 to lose weight for the final time. This time for good.

Step One – Exercise Daily for At Least Thirty Minutes

Exercise is an important component of starting up your day with your new purpose already being supported by items integrated into your routine in Phase One. Perhaps, like me, you have lost and gained weight over the past few years. Now, with your new purpose, you are ready to tackle this task with a level of intention and motivational intensity that you may have never applied before.

The day after hearing an inspirational speech that made my course clear, I put all these speeches into my playlist as I planned to start exercising again. But what was the best method to do all this? I could lift weights, do cardio, or do a myriad of so many things that would improve my physical health. How much should I exercise daily with a busy schedule of work while taking care of family and a young baby girl?

I knew from losing weight twice before that the key to successful weight loss was daily physical exercise. But what was the best way to measure all this for longer term success? When you think about all the sophisticated workout regimens and programs out there, it honestly is very overwhelming.

Below is the story of how I exercise now and why it's still part of my daily routine, no matter where I go or what I do.

Since I am a gadget and technology person, I bought an Apple Watch a long time ago for taking calls and texting people. There are three colored rings on the watch that represent standing, movement, and exercise, showing your progress during the day. If you follow the Apple system, they also recommend having a workout of higher intensity levels that lasts at least five minutes. When I started my very first walk in 2019, I thought:

> **Kirby, if you close all the rings on the Apple Watch, then this seems like a good gauge of how this part of your new routine will be.**

My goal was to do any type of activity daily without paying attention to what the rings were tracking. To get the exercise credit to close the green exercise ring, you had to do thirty minutes daily. It was summer and warm outside, so guess what I did? I simply started walking around Cary Parkway in a loop that was about two miles. This was a walk my wife and I did in 2008 together. I would put my headphones on and listen to speeches that would fill my mind with positive energy.

But what would happen when it was cold outside as the months continued? Would I still walk outside when it was bitter cold or one of the snowy or rainy days that come up in the North Carolina winter months? What about during this dark period of working for the government? Would I really want to take this final journey to lose weight despite all these things?

Part of what I learned about a strong morning routine is it emphasizes the benefits of exercise and nutrition, so I knew I was going to be on the right track doing this for my purpose. I was surprised to see other benefits beyond overall better health as I did research on this topic:

- Improved Brain Health
- Reduced Risk of Diseases
- Increased Probability of a Longer Lifespan
- Ability to Complete Daily Routine Items
- Reduced Chance of Falls

All of these things were clear in my mind, but it was item one on the list that was a game changer for me. As I started exercising in my effort to "close the rings," I could really start to feel my brain working better daily. Things were not great at this stage in the government job. I hated what I was doing, plus management made it clear they did not care about me. The time in the gym at work provided a sanctuary where I could listen to my speeches and keep my focus on strengthening my purpose.

But what about the winter weekends when I was not at work? Would I keep going even in those circumstances? This is where the lion was awakened and my ability to act was being forged in a way I never experienced up to this point in my life.

I remember one weekend day as the months got colder. It was one of the first tests to see how I would respond to my purpose. I recall it vividly, my wife looking at me like I was crazy putting on a heavy coat to do my weekend walk. My wife knew something was different if I was going to these levels to exercise. She would ask me if I wanted to just take a day off exercise on a winter weekend where we didn't go anywhere. My determination held as I focused on my purpose, rain or shine. Going back to the math equation of Intention + Motivation = Purpose, you can see why that was creating an impact.

I hope this gives some depth to the origins of the thirty minutes that are in Step One. There are many different fitness tools and trackers you can use to measure this activity. In the Apple Watch world, you only get exercise minutes when your heart rate is above a specific level, that reached at a brisk walk. So, when I closed my green ring for the day, I knew I'd put in the daily work because it was easy to measure.

What was also interesting was I never spent any money going to a gym or buying any specialized equipment then and even now. There are so many free videos and bodyweight exercises you can do online. I bought compact equipment in 2009. I started to use it during winter months after we moved into our house in 2020, but it would not all fit in the little house in Cary when we had our new baby girl because she occupied the spare room.

When I am traveling now, I try to use a hotel gym or do some walking outside if the weather is favorable. The exercise invigorates my mind and gives me time to focus on myself mentally so I can use my purpose to positively impact others.

Now let's focus on nutrition, since exercise alone wasn't the only factor in my losing weight in 2019 and being able to keep it off.

Step Two – Tracking Food Intake & Making Responsible Nutritional Choices

I listened to a great speech in the early days of my exercise commitment. There was a quote that helped me stay on track with my daily work on my physical health.

> **"The food you put into your body and everything you consume will affect your future."**

I knew that I would have to eat a lot differently, just like I did in 2002 and 2009. The Weight Watchers online system was something already proven that should work better with the right mission and purpose.

One of the reasons I like that system is that it's very technical and math based in the way it calculates how many points you can have every day. You also get points based on the level of exercise and a weekly allotment of extras you can use as you like for specific meals. For someone like me, with an engineering brain, it was always easy to latch on to this concept. Part of this goes back to the action concept of being intentional in making choices to hunt for a target.

In 2002 and 2009 I didn't have this level of intention and treated losing weight like a checkbox on a shopping list. The ability to act was there, but without a strong mission and purpose, I was very likely to go back to old habits when life circumstances were not ideal. This is what was different for me in 2019, having this strong purpose built from Phase One.

The health benefits of a consistently better diet and daily food choices have been well documented through many years of research. Companies and insurance policies have all kinds of wellness program options to help reward people who live a healthy lifestyle. Some of the known benefits from nutrition research include:

- Potential for a Longer Life
- Skin, Teeth, & Eye Health Improvement
- Muscle Health
- Overall Immunity Booster
- Lower Heart Disease or Risk of Diabetes

The first big test of my final journey through weight loss was periods of time we all struggle with:

Vacations, Family Gatherings during Holidays, & Traveling on the Road for Business.

All these periods of time in the past were very weak moments where I would say to myself that I would just "get back on the wagon" after I got back. This mindset applied to exercise as well, up until my recent weight loss in 2019.

I remember the very first cruise that my wife and I booked in Charleston, which was about one year into my most recent weight loss journey. I was doing a great job, seventy-five pounds down, and could feel myself becoming a better person with a strong purpose to never go back to who I was. Up until that trip, I was starting to think about using the gym on the ship during a vacation for the first time ever.

So here we were on board the Carnival Sunshine for the first time ever and there were so many things to see on board. Tons of shops, restaurants, casinos, bars, and opportunities to head back to my old self with possible binging during this five-day trip at sea. It was information overload with so much energy and excitement for myself and my family doing this for the first time.

Without doubt, my old self would have eaten like I did in the past and gained a lot of weight. Most people do when they go on a trip out of town. Then I would have felt guilty about self-sabotaging all the effort I put into myself because of a lack of self-worth and decisions made while out of my normal elements. But something was different this time. I was fighting the urge to make those bad decisions. It was my mission and purpose that was building up after a year of saying daily, "What I consume will affect my future."

I knew at that moment this cruise would be a turning point going forward. The first place I went to when we got settled was the gym on the ship. I did this when I had time in the evening after we had dinner. The built-up lion inside me was in action mode to keep my target in sight, no matter what was happening around me. So here I was, on a cruise ship, in the sanctuary of an elliptical machine, thinking about how I was going to plan my meal strategy while I was still in weight loss mode.

At the end of the cruise, I looked back at my intentional effort, thinking about the food and how I was going to put it in my body, and realized how much it affected my future. I did have a small setback of gaining about two pounds. Within a few days back on my home routine, I was on my way to the final leg of my destination goal. I was determined this time to not only eat right as part of my weight loss, but also to never go back to that person I used to be.

The key component again goes back to the math equation: **Intention + Motivation = Purpose**

This is why I recommend some type of nutrition plan to take care of yourself while you work on bettering your future. I am not a doctor or here to tell you how to live your life, but successful leaders are focused on having an optimized mind and body to keep their purpose strong.

You can use Weight Watchers, of course, and there are many other nutrition or weight management programs that can help achieve this area of the Morning Start Up. Some nutrition systems have meal plans you can buy online or other calorie-tracking tools. I am sure there are free tools as well to track your progress and weight. Weight Watchers Online, at the time I was writing this book, cost $20 a month. This seems like a small price for such a powerful mathematical tool I could understand with my engineering mindset. Indirectly, I used to track my exercise as well, which helped me manage my food decisions.

Application Example: Tina's Focus on her Health

One of my former beta coaching clients, Tina, was a new engineering graduate and a referral from one of my other clients. I was looking to test all the Phases of the Lion Attitude to see if this worked for other AEC professionals.

Tina was learning her way through the professional world working at a consulting engineering firm. During her college days she had a solid routine of taking care of herself physically and mentally, pretty much as how it's been outlined in this chapter.

The hustle and bustle of the working world came into play. Now suddenly there was so much to learn as a new engineer. Just like many engineers in the early days of learning their craft, she was expected to spend a lot of late nights and sometimes weekends using the drafting software, design calculations, and other tools of the trade.

Over time Tina was eating less than ideal meals. Her typical workout routine became sporadic at best, given all the new things being thrown her way. Tina told me she could feel her energy levels dropping off between the new full-time job and not really looking after her nutrition like she did in the past.

I have seen this pattern time and time again. Tina was falling into the trap of not taking care of herself in the best way possible. Her lack of intention and motivation was weakening her purpose. Tina said she started to feel physically drained at the end of every day and was running on fumes as she finished her first year of work in the professional world.

She decided to break up her day by disconnecting from work during lunchtime to spend thirty minutes exercising as I recommended. In addition, she started using some of the tracking tools to keep her physical health more optimal.

What is interesting is hearing so many people say how much energy they have after a good workout and better attention to their nutrition. Over the course of a few weeks getting settled into this new routine, Tina was really hitting a good stride. She shared that doing things spotlighted in this chapter around taking care of one's body increased her energy levels and improved her sleep. When she needed to put in a late night for some reason, she shared that sometimes she'd add a 2nd thirty-minute exercise routine to give her something different to do to help keep her mind sharp before jumping into an evening of necessary work.

My own journey with weight loss and Tina's results applying the concepts in this chapter demonstrate how important it is to take care of the body if you want it to last for a very long time with minimal issues.

Chapter 9

Journaling and Reflection

When I first heard about the concept of journaling, I thought of the old "Dear Diary" concept that people have done for many years. Usually there were items in there regarding how a person felt about someone else, or various random things that would happen daily. Those diaries and journals were some of the ways I attempted to learn how to communicate, since it was just me and a book to write how I felt about something. No time clock or concern about how exact or perfect my words would be. Just me and the journal in a quiet place, writing whatever was on my mind.

For me, even at a young age, the concept of building relationships with people was difficult. Not being able to build relationships played a key part in things not going the way I hoped or wanted. It wasn't until my mid-twenties, right after college, that I even had a relationship with a girl that lasted more than six months. The key to this goes back to leadership and the formula again:

Intention + Motivation = Purpose

Clearly, I could solve problems, which you've probably gathered from some of what's written in this book. But I didn't have the skills to do all the items in this book together until 2013. Finally, in 2019 this concept took off and changed my life. My leadership abilities changed the second I was intentional about my development. Combining this with motivation in this phase of the book created the purpose to allow me to build relationships that could stand the test of time.

Funny story is that I was cleaning out some of our furniture to move into our new house and, in the process, I found an old journal from twenty-five years ago. There were so many things I was thinking and feeling looking back. It honestly felt like I was on the other side of a mirror looking at my old self.

So here I am, going on Amazon to check out journals, expecting to find more of what I thought would be what I'd seen from my past experience. I was surprised to stumble on leadership and goal style "executive journals." The very first one that I dove into was a series of sixty-day planners. These where part of a system called the High-Performance planner. The set that I bought was a series of six journals, so I knew this was a long-term endeavor.

As I started into the journal, there were a series of questions that I needed to answer for the day. There were also the typical planner components you would expect, like tasks and scheduled meetings on the docket for the day. A section of the journal was for notes that came out of the day's reflection. I delved into this process. Something felt different about all of this versus the past. As I started the process, there were sections to label my top three targets for the day. The questions were about gratitude or reflecting on things I was doing.

This was in 2020, during my dark period of being a construction manager for the government, so my mind was focused on trying to survive the experience while I looked around for a job that aligned with my developing new purpose. There were two parts of the journal that focused on reflection, one with a morning and the other with an evening component.

I remember vividly one of the questions in the morning tied back to the importance of gratitude:

"Who is someone that did something to you which you can express gratitude for?"

Keep in mind, I had been listening to speeches that emphasized gratitude and I had this as an activity priority daily. For the first time I was working on a daily level putting all these pieces together. I was making an intentional effort to reach out to really connect with those I appreciated and thinking about all the people who supported me up to this point. I started to also realize something very deep in my heart. My lack of effort to build relationships with others put me in a position to miss all the people who likely were supporting me during many tough times of my life.

As I began the journaling process, I started to really see the impact of following all the questions every day and really thinking about what I wanted to happen. The focus of the questions in the specific journal asked about things that were wins that day, lessons learned, and how I could get better the next day. The goal behind the questions is to keep the focus on being intentional and motivated which is part of maintaining a strong purpose.

There were many days where I didn't work on everything mentioned in Phase Two that I recommend as part of the Morning Start Up. Sometimes things just don't go according to plan. However, I celebrated in a mini way each day I was putting all these steps together. Over time, I could really start to see things unfolding for me in a positive way. Journaling was something I was excited to do each evening and morning to see my growth and expansion.

On Sundays, and at the end of the month, there were weekly and monthly reflection prompts, which I would remember would take me almost an entire afternoon to complete when both of those things hit at the same time. Looking back on those days, and seeing the growth, I also realize now this was a tool to harness my already strong Intention + Motivation that my purpose was built on for my leadership development.

To this very day, I am still journaling. I have tried all kinds of products to see the differences between them. After almost four years of journaling, I think the overall goal as to why this is important is a simple pair of words: **Intention + Motivation.**

These words make up the roots of how purpose is formed. Setting a target on something and tracking it for better or worse in a journal kept me focused, even during one of the darkest periods of my professional career. It allowed me to celebrate wins but also focus with intention on the overall day at a micro level. Looking back, I think this specific part of the Morning Start Up was where I really started to see a lot of growth, which ultimately kept my motivation strong. You can see this adds up over time, building an unbreakable purpose.

If you do this daily, you will start to see the results. It was fun when the monthly review took place and I could see all these amazing things that I made happen. I was also enjoying the effect that I was having on others, which was also getting stronger.

While it was fun to celebrate the wins, I would also have days that didn't look very good. If I had an off day, I would note this as well. Or if I didn't do something in the Morning Start

Up, then I simply reflected on it during the evening time. I really started to drill down for more ways to get better with my skills during the next day with Intention + Motivation. After an off day, I woke up with a stronger focus to be better than the day before, intent on my mission and purpose.

I feel it is important to highlight some of the known physical and mental benefits of adding journaling to your morning routine:

- Improved Mental Health
- Stronger Self Confidence
- Helping Achieve Goals
- Memory Boost
- Increased Creativity
- Stronger Critical Thinking Skills
- Better Communication Skills

Let's walk through the steps on this final piece of the Morning Start Up to help you master the art of finalizing this unbreakable purpose based on Intention + Motivation.

Step One – Journal Selection Strategy

I mentioned the High-Performance planner in the beginning section of the chapter, but the ultimate message I am trying to convey is you need to be journaling with intention and motivation to accomplish something.

There are tons of "executive journals" out there that cover many types of strategies you can look at to get your morning started right. In my four years of testing out many journals, there are some that focus on specific topics like meditation, weight loss, strength training, and overall goal setting.

I want to note that the goal of the journal is not to spend 2-3 hours in the morning only on this task. You have a busy day ahead of you when you wake up, so the journal needs to be something you can put 10-15 minutes of effort in as part of your Morning Start Up.

I don't think the old-style journal, where you just write about your day overall, will have an appropriate impact as part of building your new mission and purpose. The goal is to have something that guides your intention and motivation to focus on keeping this purpose you worked so hard to build strong enough to last the test of time. You also want to wake up with energy, ready to go right after your day just like lions do when they wake up after a great night's rest.

Give yourself some space as you embark on adding this into your morning routine when you wake up. There were days where I was honestly working on this journal in the noon range of the day when my morning didn't go according to plan. The point of all this effort is to have intention and direction focused on making yourself a better person today than you were yesterday.

You also want a journal with a section to reflect on in the evening, after the day is over. The goal is to look back with a micro focus on what went well or didn't during the day. You also want to be able to review how you can get better for tomorrow, or maybe there's someone you can work with toward improving a connection with them.

After you start integrating journaling into the Morning Start Up, be sure to look at the results of who you are at the end of this phase. If you have a strong mission and purpose built in Phase One, then I am confident you will like the results across the board. Feel free to explore as many journals as you like until you find the right fit for helping you excel with your purpose.

Step Two – Daily Targets & Evening Reflection Time

All this prep in the morning sounds amazing. It seems like everything should go according to a perfect plan daily. Well, we all know that theory and reality are not always going to be the same, unfortunately.

Starting the day with an intention is the first phase of things, but where you really see the benefits is at the end of the day. The real world kicks in and suddenly, the phone calls start up and the emails come in telling you all these items that need to happen immediately, all at the same time. Think of this just like a ship heading out to sea and then out of nowhere, a storm pops up, testing your ability to keep moving forward.

For many without Intention + Motivation strengthening your purpose, your ship will sink in the storm. All the hopes you had about moving forward will be over. This is why having all the work setup in Phase One of the book is important.

Why are you putting in all this effort toward reinventing yourself from the ground up to build this purpose for your leadership?

Did you really come this far to let life put roadblocks in the way of all the dreams and goals you have towards a better life as an AEC technical professional?

The purpose you built becomes stronger with these tools. You're being tested in the blitz of all the curveballs that come up during the day.

During difficult days, it's easy to lose focus on your targets. For me, the ideal day was trying to get at least 1-2 items on the list done before even opening an email program. I typically keep my journal right beside me, so I can stay focused on those targets for the day that will have a major impact on my ultimate goals.

When the afternoon comes around, see if you can home in and try to get another target off the board. The feeling you get when you can check off major target items for the day to move the needle is incredible. Over time, you will see the impact on yourself and others around you.

However, keep in mind that not every day is going to go perfectly according to plan. You might hit one or two targets off the board instead. Regardless, you should still be celebrating your wins as you do things that move the needle, even if it's not a three for three target day. The goal comes from a speech I heard, advising everyone to have no more "Zero Days." A "Zero Day" is when you don't make any effort to move the needle at all.

Regardless of how the day ends up, whether it goes in your favor or not, make sure to disconnect from work at the end of the day. The down time focusing on family, friends, and fun things you enjoy doing will help re-energize you for the moments that make up the final part of your day. In the evenings before bed, it's the perfect time to disconnect from the electronics: TV, social media, or anything with a screen. Really look back on your day with undivided attention.

In general, look for a journal entry where you respond to the questions below:

What was something I did successfully today?
How could I get better tomorrow?
What didn't go according to plan today?
Did I learn something new today?
Who is someone who did something on my behalf I can express gratitude for?

These are some of the final things to put in your head before you lay down on the pillow. Write down all the wins, losses, people you connected with or could do a better job relating to in the future. Let them be your focus for the next day. If the day didn't go as you planned, then you get a chance to try again tomorrow with a better effort.

That gratitude mentioned in the Morning Start Up includes appreciating the ability to wake up the next day. This is something you should never take for granted. Given we might not get a chance to wake up tomorrow, try with intention to even get just 1% better today than you were yesterday.

We have reached the end of the Morning Start Up, walking through the five areas to focus on with your purpose in mind. These areas added into your morning will result in a stronger ability to develop your Intention + Motivation, creating a stronger purpose in all aspects of your day.

Now it's time to enter a final chapter item that I didn't start integrating until last year. I call this the 5am Club. Our goal behind this final chapter is to show how all five areas of the Morning Start Up work together in practice for your overall success with your new mission and purpose. Doing work on all the areas of Phase Two will have an immediate impact on your journey to develop leadership by being a strong, self-led person first.

Application Example: Rick's Top 3 Targets for the Day

I met a technical salesperson, named Rick, who I worked with after I left my role working for the government. Rick told me his day was always hectic trying to make sales calls to customers, keeping up with selections for engineers, and navigating all the internal processes that go along with sales tracking data management.

Rick explained he could spend an entire day getting caught up in emails and other communications from people needing his assistance, or him reaching out to others to collaborate. He described it as feeling like a whirlwind that never seemed to end. What really caught my attention was that he was spending all this time reacting to various things and not spending time on things that could proactively move the needle.

Over time Rick could see his ability to be intentional and motivated decreasing. Anticipating a day that was likely going to look like chaos had him feeling drained of his purpose. Constantly playing defense while reacting to others' priorities made him realize something had to change. His sales numbers were doing pretty good, but he was expending a lot of energy meeting his target quota.

Rick started asking me about journaling. I suggested a few approaches to help him start his journey. One of the journal activities that caught his attention was a section called "Top Targets." He described a section in the beginning of the journal where there were a lot of questions about what things he wanted to focus on to improve his work productivity.

After prompting the user to write down some major objectives, the journal goes into the daily pages with a list of "Top Three Targets." He told me this part of the journal was designed to focus in small steps on three things that moved the needle for some overall big goals. As part of the journal prep sections in the morning, he started to notice his time management went up a lot.

Rick's Intention + Motivation were going up as he focused primarily on things that moved the needle. Doing this gave Rick some energy. Interestingly enough, he still found strategic ways to react to things that came up during the workday. Each morning, he would get a little more energized when he could add new items to the "Top Three Targets" daily list. Over time, Rick could also see hitting each of those little targets daily was leading to more sales and less focus on items that were not really that important.

If Rick had a day that didn't go according to plan, he would reflect at night on what went wrong. His reflection kept the Intention + Motivation up so he could keep moving forward tomorrow. Usually, after deep review, Rick found solutions and iterations for correcting any patterns that were hindering his ability to keep moving the needle daily.

When Rick made this adjustment, it led to some big results in more sales, better productivity, extra energy when he hit targets during the day, and less energy focused on items that could be managed another way. Rick found out how to escape the whirlwind. Journaling was a key component to his success.

Chapter 10

Bonus Section – The 5AM Club!

The Morning Start up is based on the five chapters in this part of the book that will change the way you see your morning time before you start your day. However, a key component of this topic of starting up your day isn't something I implemented in my life until about two years ago.

My morning routine would be focused on doing all the five areas mentioned around reading, gratitude, journaling, exercise & nutrition, and meditation. However, I was getting up at 6 a.m., just in time to get our daughter up before starting my day. Most of the time I was working from home. By the time I started to work on little pieces of the Morning Start Up, it seemed like half my morning was already over.

Then I would go through the rest of my day in a mostly productive way but would still get thrown out of sync by curveballs that would come along, like a morning meeting. While I was starting to feel the impact of adding the Morning Start Up, it didn't feel like it was having the greatest possible optimized effect. And then I started listening to different speakers and speeches that caused me to realize I needed to start getting up earlier in the day.

There have been a lot of studies that indicate being up earlier in the morning will create a bigger impact on your day. I did a lot of research and discovered successful executives got up in the morning around 4-6 a.m.

Once again, my engineering brain pondered this concept and concluded if all these successful people were doing this, I should adopt it as well.

I can say out of all the things I have mentioned in Phase Two of this book, this was the hardest thing to do. When I first started this final piece, it was brutal. I even found myself partially falling back asleep. My brain was thinking I was a crazy person to be up an extra hour earlier, an hour before I had to get my daughter ready for daycare. It took a solid one to two months before I got into the rhythm of waking up at 5 a.m.

Then I started to see the impact in my day. During that extra hour I had time to meditate, journal, and send a gratitude message to someone so they saw it first thing in their day. I had time to read books and really develop a strong intention for my day. I didn't have time to exercise but did that immediately after getting the little one ready while my wife left for the day. In the summer I go for a morning walk and am ready by 8 a.m. to start my workday.

It's amazing that simply getting up one hour earlier than I did previously would make so much of a difference in my entire day overall. Let's start with some strategy on how to integrate the final piece and tie the Morning Start Up together into a system to impact your day with more clarity and intention.

Step One – Wind Down Routine

A lot of emphasis is placed on how important a strong morning routine is for your day. Getting up at 5 a.m. helps you to be intentional about taking care of yourself before starting your workday. However, this is honestly easier said than done.

One of the things I struggled with was being able to see what the end of my day would look like. As I was fighting the process of getting up early with my brain, the biggest issue was a proper getting to bed process.

As a father taking care of a then baby/toddler daughter, my bedtime process was very erratic at best. We would make every effort to get her in bed as a then three-year-old. Getting a child ready for bed is in some ways like herding cats. I would usually be the one staying up to make sure the little girl was in bed so my wife could get some extra rest after a long day teaching elementary school. These nights always tested my patience. It was hard watching a little one come out of the bedroom, making any chance of a wind down time for me impossible. There were also many nights when she'd wake up after wetting the bed during the potty-training phase. I would go to bed mentally exhausted from an intentional day and morning without really being able to shut things off.

I started to look back at why it was so hard to get up at 5 a.m. One difference that helped was that our little one got older. It was a lot easier to manage making sure she went to bed on time, since we didn't have to watch her as much as we did during her toddler years. Of course, like many people, I was scrolling on my phone or computer nearly right up to the point of bedtime.

I figured out this missing link was not initiating a proper wind down time before going to bed.

Establishing a proper routine before going to bed is just as important as waking up with a good plan for starting the day. Here are some of the strategies I recommend you consider making as part of your wind down routine:

- Evening Meditation Session
- No Phone Screen Time Thirty Minutes Before Bedtime
- Additional Reading in Bed for Fifteen Minutes
- Breathing Exercises
- No Electronics in the Bedroom

As I started to work on these items, adding them into my bedtime wind down, it suddenly became a lot easier to wake up. I felt like my sleep quality was improving a lot, based on measurement tools I was using, like my Withings Sleep device. The better wind down routine strategy also reduced the number of times I was up in the middle of night. Gone are the 3 a.m. racing mind mornings when I couldn't get back to sleep.

Over time I was starting to enjoy the early morning time. That one extra hour is a sanctuary for me to be by myself. The wind down each evening helps me sleep well and be able to get up easily at 5 a.m. I can tell the difference when I must go to bed without winding down. It makes it a lot more mentally challenging to stay focused the next day.

Step Two – How Many Hours of Sleep Should I Get?

While crafting the Morning Start Up strategy, I did a lot of research on the executive world. My plan was to see how they started up their day, but I was also surprised to discover when they went to bed. There are many studies out there that recommend at least 7-9 hours of sleep a day. If you put this 5 a.m. wake-up time into calculations, it would result in a bedtime of 8-10 p.m.

Not getting enough sleep has a cascading effect that will impair your ability to think and function properly over time. The ability to manage emotions becomes a lot more difficult as well. I was also surprised to see a lack of sleep had the additional adverse effects:

- Obesity
- Diabetes
- Hypertension
- Anxiety

It has been interesting to see so much research around getting quality sleep. You see NFL commercials now of players walking through the process of how they are measuring all the data to maximize their rest. I was also surprised to read that so many executives were getting 7-9 hours of sleep a night.

What I realized was executives are not these crazy people working 20+ hour days to advance their careers or run their own businesses. They get up early in the morning, have great wind down routines, and are then able to get to bed at a good time so they can get the right amount of targeted sleep on a consistent basis.

Seeing this research was honestly the biggest relief for me. What I started to realize was that all this routine was also indirectly teaching me a form of time management away from work. We have read about all kinds of time blocking options that are for the workday, but what about before and afterwards?

Application Example: Tim's 3rd Shift Version of the 5AM Club

I wanted to give a little different twist in application on the 5AM Club, since not everyone is always working the typical 8 a.m. to 5 p.m. desk job. The AEC industry is filled with people who have various responsibilities in manufacturing, logistics, and road construction.

Not every project can be done during the typical business hours because owners' requirements sometimes mean some part of a project needs to stay operational 24/7. As a result, many people must work on the 2nd or 3rd shift as their unusual work hours. I hope this example provides another clear differentiator between the AEC industry in comparison to other fields.

Tim was a supervisor for a roadway crew that does horizontal construction with roads. He told me a lot of stories about how difficult it is to maintain a normal schedule when you are working 3rd shift. It takes a long time to get used to sleeping during the day. It can be even harder to have a start-up routine to keep your Intention + Motivation going, even when you've established a strong purpose. By the end of his shift, the sun would just be coming up and he'd be on his way home, totally exhausted.

When I thought about the 5AM Club, a person like Tim honestly never crossed my mind. Tim has as much ambition to build his skills in the construction world as anyone else. I started to think about Tim after I was doing the Morning Start Up presentations, trying to figure out how this could apply to someone in our field who doesn't work a normal shift.

In Tim's case, we discussed potentially splitting aspects of the Morning Start Up into two sections. The idea was that he would get up about an hour earlier than usual so he could do the quicker-paced things like the journaling, reading, and some meditation. During those three activities, he would also be thinking about someone whom he could send a quick email to, expressing gratitude as part of making someone else's day brighter.

Off Tim went to work with a little extra focus (Intention + Motivation) on making his day successful, even though his day was doing a hard night's worth of labor on the jobsite. He told me that just doing most of the start-up tasks really helped keep his purpose strong, which included his belief that working these odd hours would eventually benefit his future.

When it came time for his wind down before bed, he would enjoy a nice evening workout, either walking or going to the gym to keep his energy level up. Tim told me that taking the exercise component out of the morning routine and moving to his end of the day activities gave him some of the benefits I was describing, based on my own routine.

The application example of Tim is a highlight that the goal behind the 5AM Club is developing an intentional and motivated focus on making extra effort to prep yourself for your day. In the next chapter, I will be sharing my version of the Morning Start Up and also how the 5AM Club works for me.

Chapter 11

Final Closing – Example of Kirby's Typical Morning

We have tied together a lot of concepts here in this part of the book. When you start to slowly work your way toward integrating items from the book into your daily activities, the Morning Start Up will eventually become habit. To put this in perspective, I recommend installing this incrementally, working through a little at a time for about a three-month period to put all the items into play daily.

For many people, there will be some things you've already executed. If this is the case, then that's excellent. You have a head start on integrating the remaining items as part of your day and evenings.

I wanted to show a typical day for me so you can get a visual in practice to see what things look like putting it all together. Note that when I am traveling, some days it's easier to start up than others, but give yourself some grace here. If you fall down, you have to get right back up and keep moving forward. Remember that lions fail at getting targets daily, but that doesn't stop them from moving forward to hunt for their targets again.

Kirby's typical day

Wake Up: 5:00 a.m.

Meditation: 5:15 a.m.

Journaling: 5:45 a.m.

Reading: 6:15 a.m.

Wake Up Daughter & Take to School: 7:00 a.m.

Exercise: 7:30 a.m.

Start of Workday: 8:00 a.m.

End of Workday: 5:00 p.m.

Family Time: 7:30 p.m.

Light Work/Development Projects: 8:15 p.m.

Daughter's Bedtime: 8:30 p.m.

Evening Journaling Reflection/Wind Down Time/Personal Development: 8:30 – 9:00 p.m.

Bedtime Target: 9:00 to 10:00 p.m.

Total Sleep: 7-8 hours

In closing, I hope all of this is helpful. It's now time to enter Phase Three of the Lion Attitude journey to master the concepts of Action + Connection based on the purpose you built in Phase One and Two. The next phase of the book is where you really get to see how to harness the power of the lion's core attributes into your leadership development. The focus will now be on applying leadership skills toward working with others, since the self-leadership work is done.

Let our journey keep going, hunting after targets like lions in the wild.

Phase 3

Outer Leadership –
Lion Attribute Integration

Phases One and Two were about developing your purpose and then enhancing it with daily focus in the Morning Start Up based on Intention + Motivation. It takes strong self-leadership as an AEC professional to tackle the upcoming Phases of Three and Four, but you are ready for this task.

The focus of Phase Three is on the application of your purpose as it relates to building leadership skills for working with others using the concept of Action + Connection. Did you know lions are one of the only apex predators in the entire world that have the special talent to be elite at Action + Connection at the same time?

A lion possesses masterful levels of vision, decision making, acumen, risk taking, and strategy (action). These abilities allow him to hunt in a way that no other animal can, even without specific natural advantages. Elephants are bigger than lions. Cheetahs are faster than lions. Based on this logic, these bigger, faster animals should be apex predators and kings of the jungle, correct?

What they don't have is the power of connection, which lions present and build at masterful levels. Lions operate in prides with a very specific system in which they work together, build meaningful relationships, and live, growing stronger as a family (connection). It's interesting to consider a 600-pound killing machine is also one of the most social animals in the world.

When you look at this overall, you can see that lions have a strong ability to Act + Connect. Looking back on some of the best leaders I have seen in the AEC industry, they all had this Act + Connect concept in common, just like lions.

But how is this possible and what traits does it take to perform at the level that lions do as a leader?

In Phase One I shared the five words that changed everything for me: courage, strength, bravery, leadership, and heart. It's these five areas we want to focus on for leadership development. Building these skills allows us to develop leadership skills using the ability to Act + Connect every day, like lions in the wild.

The goal is to focus on application of our reinvention & purpose development (Phase One) combined with daily self-development (The Morning Start Up – Phase Two) to Act + Connect, mastering the five lion attributes below:

Courage, Strength, Bravery, Leadership, & Heart

When you look at each of these leadership development focus areas, some seem more like action traits, while others are more about connection. Each chapter will help you learn how to work on integrating a balance of Action + Connection into your professional and business development. This will allow you to harness that power of the lion inside you to change yourself. Your transformation will affect others around you in meaningful ways.

But before we delve into these five attributes, I want to explain why it's so important to master the ability in your leadership of Act + Connect simultaneously. Focusing on only one or the other doesn't work. Through examples, I'll illustrate what happens when someone pays attention to only one side of the spectrum. Then we will go into the five attributes of a lion to explore strategies on how to use your new purpose built in Phase One, combined with a strong intentional morning routine in Phase Two, to become like a lion leader in the AEC industry.

Application Example: Action Only Approach – The Attacker

I have encountered a lot of salespeople over my professional career in Architecture/ Engineering/Construction and one thing is for certain:

Technical salespeople who are 100% commissioned sellers show strong tendencies of pure attackers.

In their world, time is valuable. When you are a salesperson, you must make sales to generate income to survive. This requires a daily strategy to win jobs when it comes to bid day. Then, after an order is placed, there is a micro level of focus on what's going on at the factory. Technical salespeople want to communicate every detail with end customers, the owners, engineers, and contractors. This encourages an attack mindset and strategy of winning jobs that results in more orders, and ultimately, more income.

When a salesperson hits a big win, it's a big accomplishment. Sadly, it's a feeling they only get to enjoy for maybe a day or two, tops. That's because they still must keep the pipeline flowing to hit their sales targets. They still must spend time learning about the products and understanding weak and strong points of what they are selling. Working as part of a team is usually not a focus for a salesperson, but they still need to manage internal company relationships.

One would think that a pure attacker mindset would be a strength, right? Unfortunately, that's rarely true. Here's an example of a memorable incident:

I was working with a salesperson who had an issue with a project's piece of equipment. The unit arrived on site with all kinds of problems. These had been discovered in the field months ago. Finally, the root cause was determined to be a major factory defect. Consequently, a completely new unit had to be built.

I took the lead on communication that took place two to three times a day to resolve this issue. At the same time, I was also working with our internal factory team for input and updates, given this very dire set of circumstances requiring a unit replacement. In the current world, supply chain orders get delayed frequently due to component and labor shortages. This has affected the entire design and construction world, and still does to this very day. The factory team went above and beyond to find a replacement to meet the client's needs in record time.

I had gotten the news on Thursday that the unit was ready for shipment and felt relief hearing it was coming. After a lot of high intensity efforts over nearly four straight days that ran into evenings working with this salesperson, I was ready to work on less intense things for a little bit. Then on Friday afternoon, I got a call that a delivery appointment was missed. This was a major red flag. I made some calls trying to understand what happened. I discovered the person who promised the delivery date didn't schedule the unit to be shipped. The tragic news was this individual had just found out a person in their family was hospitalized and not going to survive, so they forgot to finish the order delivery details. Our shipping lead placed a call and coordinated rescheduling of the delivery to correct the issue.

How the salesperson reacted is something I will never forget. He got very upset and wrote the following words in an email on a Friday afternoon to me:

"This is ridiculous. How can we ever sell equipment after this fiasco, Kirby?"

This salesperson was only focused on attacking at this moment and wasn't using any ability to connect. Knowing the reason was due to a shipping coordinator having a death in the family made me feel a level of empathy I had finally started to understand in recent years. I felt anger inside me for weeks and even months afterwards, knowing how hard the factory team worked to help this customer. This salesperson showed zero empathy and failed to engage teamwork to solve the issue. I never told anyone other than my wife, and later, a now former colleague who I have a high level of respect for.

My response to this salesperson was:

"The person who scheduled made an error due to a family member's death. I would have hoped you'd show a little more human compassion and are better than what you just sent to me."

You can see that focusing only on action will transform you into being an attacker. This means your decisions and actions are all self-focused only on results to win at the expense of hurting others in the process. Sometimes you win and don't even realize how many people you hurt. This is even worse.

People in "manager" roles who behave as attackers may show these tendencies:

- Taking credit for team members' work instead of highlighting the team first.
- Blaming team members and not taking ownership as the leader from a total responsibility standpoint.
- Showing no empathy for people or team members.

As a result, the people around them disconnect and distance themselves from the attacker. The team will never show any loyalty to an attacker, since they know this is someone who will not have their back when things get hard.

A leadership executive wanted to meet with me in Oklahoma regarding what took place over this rooftop unit. As I shared more about this experience with him concerning the heartless salesperson, he said something that's stuck with me. The executive explained that the mindset of aggressive salespeople as attackers usually results in leaving behind a lot of bodies in the process. They celebrate their individual wins, but the feeling ends up being very hollow when it costs others along the way.

I never spoke with that salesperson after that Friday afternoon. I'm not sure what I would say if I did see him face-to-face. That was a dark moment for me, but it led to a lot of great things afterwards. This included the realization of how important it is to focus on Action + Connection while implementing the five lion attributes.

However, only being a connector isn't a good solution either.

Application Example: Connector Only Approach – The Con Artist

While attackers are obvious with their impact on others, both positive and negative, the pure connector gets a special name that's not something to be proud about: con artist.

Con artists have very strong social and relationship skills, are very difficult to immediately detect, and are able to blend into any room and make friends easily. They usually look like the life of the party and seem like they have everything you could imagine at their fingertips. I would look at these people for many years of my life with nothing but jealousy because they had these abilities.

Con artists are not able to execute plans or make things a reality. Their focus is solely on relationships, having fun, and blending in with crowds seamlessly. However, when it comes time to get them to develop a plan of action, share a vision, or put in the effort on a consistent basis to make something a reality, they don't have the ability to deliver actual results. My next story highlights the impact a con artist has on others.

When I was traveling in Mississippi recently, I had a conversation with a salesperson and an owner's rep for a school system at a dinner meeting. As a person who's worked for the government as an owner's rep, it's interesting to learn how the internal workings of design and construction are different from my experience.

The person at our dinner meeting had worked his way up through the ranks in facilities management and was involved in HVAC maintenance on buildings in the school system. As he got promoted a few times, he advanced into leadership roles where he was managing technicians who were taking care of school system facilities.

We were having a conversation about con artists and he immediately went into vivid detail about an employee under his wing who fit this mold. The technician had a big personality and was very people friendly. This allowed him to build relationships with local teachers and principals at schools where he did the maintenance. The owner's rep mentioned that he would go by and check every so often to see how things were going, plus do a walkthrough of the facilities to see how he could help his staff get better.

For this specific technician, he noticed that each time he would do a walkthrough, there would be items that were not fixed. The supervisor would ask each time why certain items had not been fixed yet. The technician would make up all kinds of reasons why and would try to use his strong connection skills to deflect these comments concerning his lack of results. Eventually, the supervisor lost trust and confidence in this person, doubting he could do the jobs assigned for delivery to the school system.

Ultimately the person was transferred out into a smaller role doing something else. It cost him an opportunity for higher level roles coming up in the future. Granted, this took a while, but you can see the results of the con artist are not really any different than a pure attacker. They're ineffective.

People in "manager" roles who behave as con artists usually show these tendencies:

- Not being able to execute a plan on how to accomplish something.

- Will not roll up their sleeves to work with a team to resolve issues. This is likely due to the fact they don't know anything or have any ability to understand the work required to accomplish a task.

- Will share a vision on how to do something that has no chance of success.

The goal behind integrating the five lion attributes of courage, strength, bravery, leadership, and heart is to teach you skills to develop leadership as a technical professional. It's important to understand how the concepts of Action + Connection work together, using the strong purpose you developed earlier. Being effective in only one of these areas is not going to work. I have highlighted real world examples of this so you can see the impact of being one dimensional with your leadership development.

Let's begin with the first lion attribute to develop and apply as part of your leadership development working with other people. Remember the goal is Action + Connection together to develop outer leadership in Phase Three, not Attacking + Conning people.

Chapter 12

Courage Development & Strategy

A great Les Brown speech I listened to a few years ago mentioned that courage comes from French origins. In France this term means "of the heart." Les mentions how courage is formed from the heart. It seems fitting that courage and heart are tied together, given the importance of harnessing the concepts of Action + Connection as we delve into this subject.

In the traditional dictionary, courage is defined as having the fear of something, but still moving forward with it anyway. We all face fears in our life that come in many forms. These can be physical, mental, or emotional. The sense of not having strong purpose augments these fears even further, to the point where it seems like nearly everything is impossible. This is why we focus on developing a strong rooted purpose first, built to give confidence in all the work you've started in Phase One and Two of this book. This will serve you well as you work through more steps in the Lion Attitude process.

The first test in life is starting to stare down into your fears, moving forward even with the smallest steps. At this point, confidence should start flowing. You'll sense it's time to tackle something in your life that you have been putting off for a while. But what should you start with first?

My recommendation is targeting your top three fears in physical, emotional, and mental obstacle areas and write them down. These should be important obstacles in your life which you can overcome. Your goal in this part is being able to look at your fears now with purpose that you didn't have before. By being intentional and motivated you can generate the purpose to overcome your worse fears while developing courage.

So now that you have those top three fears in your mind, it's time to write them down on a dry erase board so you can see them daily. Below is a good guide to examples of courage in all three areas mentioned. If you're stuck on what you might be afraid of, look up phobia lists online to get ideas that apply to your concerns.

Physical Courage - Overcoming Fear of Heights, Medical Appointments, Needles

Mental Courage - Overcoming Fear of Self Confidence Issues & Self Worth

Emotional Courage - Standing up for Something you Believe in Even if by Yourself; Standing up to Someone who is a Bully or Hurtful

The goal behind this part is to make you ready to step into your fears and come out on the other side of this as a different person. Note that we will be covering the difference between courage and bravery later, but the key component is the level of risk involved. Acts of courage usually do not involve risking something significant, like your life.

Over the course of a week, take a deep look at yourself. Start to write down those fears you have when you are at this stage in the system. You only need to tackle one of the three, so take your pick in any of the areas listed above. After you complete this major accomplishment, notice how you feel afterwards.

Below is a specific example where I felt the power of courage as well as its impact afterwards.

Application Example: Lisa's Decision to Ask for a Raise

During my time as a consulting engineer, I met Lisa, who was a client working at an architecture firm we did business with. At the time I met Lisa, she was an architectural designer and working through the process to become a fully licensed architect.

In the Architecture/Engineering (A/E) world, design professionals are billed out at an hourly rate, then actual wages can either be in the form of an hourly rate or as a salary. In the design side of the AEC business, A/E professionals can only bill time based on their knowledge, skill level, and expertise.

Many people in the A/E world spend a lot of time preparing and studying for the professional exams.

> **Becoming licensed usually results in a substantial raise as a now registered architect/engineer.**

Lisa had been studying for a while to prepare for all the exams and the process of licensure. I saw her hard work and dedication. She was spending time in the evenings on preparations for getting licensed while also managing a full-time job during the day. As Lisa was going through the process, I was encouraging her, sending messages about how all this effort and short-term sacrifice of time was going to be worth it down the road.

I noticed that Lisa was out for about a week after we had wrapped up a project together and was curious how things went on the exams. There was something different in her email signature when she got back that I immediately noticed:

Registered Architect

I called Lisa congratulating her for this significant and life-altering accomplishment. She was excited and took some time off to celebrate with family and friends after finding out she'd passed. Lisa was on top of the world and everything pointed to it being a smooth ride for transition into a new role at her firm.

Lisa figured passing this exam meant she was going to get a big raise. I told her I expected her principal at the company to approach her quickly about raising her compensation, since she was now billing out at a much higher level than she could as a designer.

A few weeks went by. Little was different for Lisa other than her working through the process of completing her paperwork for delivery of her license and registration, and added responsibility. Her principal at the company discussed having her take on more of a lead role on some projects. She was also given permission to get junior level staff involved in jobs to help her grow into her new role.

After about a month of these adjustments, Lisa felt something was a little off about this situation. Her principal at the firm still hadn't scheduled a meeting to discuss her new salary after passing the licensure exam. She didn't feel right about being paid a designer's wage while being shouldered with the additional responsibility given to registered architects. Was her supervisor going to reach out to discuss this important item in the future?

Any time you decide to ask the head of a company for a raise you face uncertainty. Most people in the AEC industry, and in other industry workforces, feel a gut full of fear when considering the potential outcome of a conversation of this magnitude.

What if this principal Lisa worked for said no?

What if she didn't get what she'd determined was her market value after doing research prior to this conversation to support her request?

What if this was not the right time to ask because the company was not doing well financially right now?

Lisa was feeling deep fear about this situation physically, mentally, and emotionally as each day went by. She waited for her principal to approach her to discuss her new licensure, billing rate, and new responsibilities.

Lisa had done all the inner leadership steps in Phase One and Two, building a purpose and harnessing it with Intention + Motivation daily. Now she was facing a big test of courage to see if she could focus on developing her ability to act on moving forward to overcome this situation.

Finally, nearly two months later, Lisa told me she was going to meet with her principal at the firm and discuss the change in her compensation. The research Lisa did to determine her market value included talking to recruiters. She also spent time preparing her remarks and reciting them. The night before started to visualize what the outcome would look like in any scenario she could think of. She decided she was going to overcome the fear of all of this and move forward, regardless of the meeting outcome. If all this didn't work out, she knew she could land a role at a competing company, getting the compensation she deserved.

I remember when Lisa told me she was going to have this conversation. I really cared about her and wanted nothing but the best. I told her to message me later in the evening after everything was over.

Lisa was afraid of all the things that could go wrong during this meeting. However, she was developing the courage to move forward regardless of what her boss said. Lisa felt very empowered by her preparation around asking for a raise. She had an action strategy for every possible scenario. Lisa needed to have strong inner leadership based on intention, motivation, and purpose to develop courage. After she had a long conversation with her principal, I got this message from her:

> **"Kirby, I got the raise I wanted to match the market rate I hoped for that aligns with my new role and responsibility as a registered architect! This is one of the greatest days for me that I will never forget."**

Lisa provides a great example of overcoming a fear and the results of what happens when you move forward despite what could happen. When you get on the other side of courage, you feel amazing, just like Lisa did in this application.

This highlights why courage is so important for people in professional and leadership development. We all have mental, physical, and emotional fears that we will face in life, but to become a different person, our purpose must push us beyond those fears. All the work in Phase One and Two gets you ready for this moment of truth.

This is the Action + Connection mindset we develop with courage to push on regardless of the circumstances or fears you face. The action part takes the initiative to overcome your fears and the connection delves into the origins of what made you afraid of them to begin with. Harnessing and mastering your ability in Action + Connection together will be the reason you are now in control of your fears and not the other way around. It's still okay to be afraid, but you must keep moving forward no matter what.

Now let's use this new reinvented version of courage to develop strength.

Chapter 13

Strength Development & Strategy

When we think about strength, the first thing that automatically comes to mind is the physical side of things. The easiest analogy to building our inner strength is what takes place when you head to the gym and exercise. This is part of the Morning Start Up in Phase Two. Your body is being reconditioned and tested with resistance, which makes your body stronger over time. At some point, the resistance becomes less, due to increased strength. As a result of the new strength developed, you must add additional resistance to keep growing and being even stronger than you are now. This comes with developing new skills.

If you think about this on the mental and emotional level, the same concepts apply. You must put your mind and feelings through resistance to get stronger in situations which result in more growth and development. Below are some areas of strength to focus on which can help make you better as a technical professional.

<u>Physical Strength</u> – Gaining Muscle and Toning Your Body to Improve Stamina and a Feeling of Wellbeing

<u>Mental Strength</u> – Taking Extra Classes/Education/Certifications

<u>Emotional Strength</u> – Working on Areas of Emotional Intelligence (EQ) like Self-Awareness, Self-Management, Social Awareness, Relationship Management

We cover the concept of strength development in your courage relative to how you will feel when you face your first fears head on. Think about how you felt after overcoming one of your fears. Lisa's moment of victory in asking for a raise and getting it from her principal gave her the power to get stronger, which exponentially increased her confidence.

People who apply courage to conquering a fear usually see more potential for additional growth afterwards. Your confidence gets sky high. Once you face your internal fears head on, you start to see your abilities as being strong enough to do just about anything. Building courage is an important first step in creating an unbreakable purpose in Phase One and Two. It's only natural that people tackle next steps with more confidence after a victory, enough to make developing your bigger goals a reality.

The key component of this part of the journey in attaining your strength goal is building on the ability to harness your Action + Connection skills. It takes effort, planning, and strategy to grow and get stronger, which is where the ability for action gets developed. You will also feel more able to connect during this process. Working with other people to get stronger builds bonds and relationships which results in wins for your entire lion pride.

So now it's time to take a deep look into what strengths you want to grow and develop to help take you to another level. Don't spend a lot of time focused on several fears at once. Just pick one. This will be the poster child for your new self to keep moving forward.

Lions in the wild work daily to keep growing and developing to get stronger so they can be the apex predator in the wild. Here's an application example journey with the focus on strength:

Application Example: Amanda's Switch from Engineer to Owner's Representative

Amanda, a person I used to work with, had been an engineer in the AEC industry for a very long time. She was employed at a lot of great companies and was very savvy from a technical perspective, working her way to the top in her field. However, something felt different after getting to the top. She didn't feel challenged anymore.

Amanda was worn down from the hustle and bustle of all the endless hours working as a consulting engineer. She started to explore different AEC fields where her skill sets would be appreciated. Her goal was to find a role suited to her engineering background where she could grow and continue to get stronger. It's not uncommon to see people in AEC parts of the business switch from one position to another, for various reasons.

It didn't take long. Amanda found an opportunity with a private developer as a construction manager for the owner, who had a lot of new buildings and associated growth in the area. She had been on the design front her entire career, where she went to job sites to monitor progress in construction. During her time exploring a career shift, she asked owner's representatives a lot of different questions about their perspective from a different vantage point.

Amanda was excited about the change of pace and different project point of view. Taking the owner's rep role meant a better work/life balance. She had more time flexibility to better support her family as issues came up. However, Amanda knew there would be some challenges and many new things to learn requiring strength as she strove to improve herself during the career pivot transition.

This new role required a lot of administrative duties as part of her putting together bid packages for architects, engineers, and contractors as a construction manager. Suddenly, many of the technical skills she had used for years didn't apply to her work as an owner's representative.

She did find a major strength in her prior experience during design reviews on projects. But now she was relying on other people to solve problems for her. Amanda found herself struggling emotionally with her lack of skills and perspectives needed to solve unfamiliar problems for the owner.

Amanda was also expected to manage construction budgets and keep up with developing issues at the jobsites. There were many things that came up in her early projects that she hadn't encountered as a consulting engineer previously. During her time as an engineer, she was peripherally concerned about budgets, but now paying close attention to the numbers was a critical concern for success in her new role.

Deep down Amanada knew it was going to take a lot of growth and strength to learn necessary skills for her new role. Her first project involved working on a tenant upfit on a floor in one of the buildings the developer owned. This opportunity was a prime example of how much strength she needed growing into an owner's rep construction manager.

For some this pivot might seem like an impossible task. Action is a major component of strength development. Amanda was determined to make this work. She was spending time taking project management classes to master new skills. She was also learning how to navigate the switchover and relying on other paid consultants to solve the issues, where before, in her engineer roles, she'd simply try to figure out solutions by herself.

When the tenant upfit was over, she felt a big sense of accomplishment and growth from working to get stronger in her career pivot skill advancement. Now Amanda's new talents could be used to make her a better overall AEC professional in the industry. The key component of all this was the action and effort it took to make her focus on strength become a reality. She combined this with connection and appreciation for working with architects, engineers, and contractors to gain from different perspectives.

You'll feel a rush of energy when you complete the strength leg of the journey. The growth and expansion yield big dividends in the long run. But what it also revealed to me is we are more capable of choosing to get better than we ever imagined. Strength is built from hard work and effort, which is the reason Amanda was proud of her first project as a new owner's representative.

You can see in this application example that working on strength required a heavy dose of action for Amanda. But she also needed connection, which was formed by all the people who supported her during the journey to get better.

Outer leadership comes by taking the initiative to get better as a professional with our lion pride cheering on as we work to grow as AEC professionals.

A quick little note, but another easy example of strength for me personally in 2023: **writing this book, *The Lion Attitude.***

Chapter 14

Bravery Development & Strategy

This is the midpoint of our journey through the integration of the attributes of lions. I hope at this point you can start to feel the development of the ability to Act + Connect working through each of the chapters in Phase Three.

It's part of your development to be able to Act + Connect working on outer leadership skills with other people. However, the toughest test comes at the mid-point of lion attribute integration. You have built the confidence in overcoming something with courage and worked to grow yourself with some skills that make you stronger. The journey to develop bravery will be the biggest challenge you will face heading into the back half of the attribute integration process. But let's take a step backwards and review a key item that comes up a lot.

Many people assume that courage and bravery are the same thing. While they are linked, there is a big difference between the two. The biggest is related to the concept of fear. The first thing I thought when reviewing the definition of bravery was the ultimate example of firefighters and their training to be able to run into a burning building. When you see the imagery of a firefighter doing this feat, the key component is showing zero fear during this heroic act. The goal of the firefighter running into the building is to put their own life on the line to save someone else's.

While it is clearly a brave effort as this moment takes place, when fire-fighters enter the building to save a life, there are major calculated risks done well before that moment in time as part of this decision-making process. Think of all the training and safety checks being done daily at the firehouse where no one is watching. Firefighters are training and developing themselves daily to make sure the risks they take are a calculated gamble designed to work out in their favor. If they show any ounce of fear during those moments, many people's lives could be at stake, so they must be able to act with no hesitation.

Courage needs to be developed before you can make good progress in the bravery category, so this is why we focus the attribute integration in this specific order. But there are acts of bravery that happen with lions as well when they hunt in the wild. They take lots of calculated risks with decisions when hunting to be able to have zero fear going after targets. One moment of hesitation could be the difference between getting a target in the wild or getting taken out by another animal. Lions take big risks, but as a result, the rewards are far more substantial than they would be if they didn't.

But bravery, just like the other attributes, can be developed in multiple ways. I give examples of each area below:

Physical Bravery – Sports athletes risk themselves when injured, continuing to play for the team to help them win.

Mental Bravery – A professional decides to quit their job to start a business working for themselves full time. The risk involves possible financial implications that could impact themselves or their family. The potential reward is to gain a lifestyle far greater than what's available by simply taking a typical job at a company.

Emotional Bravery – Standing up for yourself in a workplace for something that puts your job in jeopardy, or defending something you believe in, even with no support around you. The risk is high, where you could lose a lot of things in the future, but it could create an impact far beyond just you in that moment.

I recommend you take about a week to really look at yourself again in the mirror. Something to keep in mind when it comes to bravery is that a lot of thought and strategy comes into play when you are taking a risk of this magnitude. Being brave is important, but you must also avoid being reckless with decision-making on this part of the journey.

I think of this moment like sitting in a casino, gambling at the table, taking a risk where you are looking at a strategy for the highest chances to win. I don't think going to the roulette wheel and putting all your life savings on the green 00 number is going to typically result in a big win. Yes, you could really win something big by taking this kind of risk, but the odds are about as good as trying to hit the Powerball. We all know how that usually turns out.

What is something that you want to pursue where you are willing to risk something substantial with zero fear in hopes of getting a big return?

Application Example: Kirby's Bet on Triangle ASHRAE Team for a Fall Research Fundraiser at Drive Shack

The Triangle ASHRAE Chapter had a profound impact on my life during the eighteen months I was President of the group. I vividly remember a specific moment took place during my second term. Our team was a well-built machine up to this point and consistently ranked in the top performers in comparison to all 190+ chapters in the world. I will share more in the Leadership section, but I wanted to touch on the later part of my term here. Something came out of my last half year that was one of the biggest examples of bravery during my journey to rebuild myself from scratch.

Our Triangle team had been looking at different events for the fall to support ASHRAE research. To give some background, ASHRAE is a non-profit organization that is supported mostly by volunteers who gather to help develop codes and standards to support the HVAC and built environment. Lots of volunteers devote time, traveling resources, and effort to sit on committees to support these updated standards. The standards are updated based on having industry supporters from all different perspectives like contractors, owners, engineers, manufacturers, and policy makers. The key function is having scientific research to support fact and data-based decisions. An ASHRAE chapter's role in this process is to help raise money for research projects that play a major role in the funding to support standard updates.

We headed into our ASHRAE year on July 1, 2019, right after I started my reinvention process. I was organizing the initial planning meetings as part of the year so we could have a solid strategy to make this year one of the best the chapter ever had in its history. We have typically done two research promotion fundraising events a year, with one during the spring and the other in the fall.

Our spring event has been a golf tournament, which was wildly successful for many years and resulted in significant profits for funding our ASHRAE research goal target for the year. However, our fall event was changed a few years back into a 5K fun run. Momentum was starting to decline at the event after a big turnout three years prior. Looking back at the event, the attendance kept going down each year, and along with it, the energy levels of our team. During the year which I ended up taking over as President, we did the final 5K fun run halfway through my term. The event had the lowest attendance in recent years. At the end of the event our team agreed we needed to do something different. What we ended up doing would be one of my biggest moments in finding my bravery.

I had a flash back about one of the first trips I ever took for professional development for my engineering license. It was in Dallas, Texas to see Titus HVAC. This is a company that focuses on grilles, registers, and diffusers, along with other types of air movement devices. When I made this trip in 2013, something that really stood out to me was a fun evening going to a place called Topgolf for social time.

Topgolf is a driving range on steroids, with all kinds of lighted targets to hit. It also has good food in a relaxed environment. Typical driving ranges I used to head to as a kid with my dad were outside and only really something we did together during the summer. There is no way I would have considered going to a place like one of these in the cold of winter. This is where Topgolf was different. All the bays in the typical three stories were heated. You could play year-round on the range, if you wanted to, in total comfort.

There were various target games you could play all over the range. You could shoot for accuracy then break out the driver, blasting balls as hard as possible to hit the back of the net around 250 yards away. I think during my entire time ever going to places like this, I might have seen one or two people able to hit the ball hard enough to reach the back of the net.

While going to the golf range and hitting balls was a fun thing to do with my dad, it was nothing that ever amounted to my getting interested in going to an actual golf course. Yet, here I was, having a blast hitting balls and watching the flight tracker as I hit targets everywhere at all kinds of distances. This was the most fun golf experience that I ever had up to this point in my life. I found myself yearning to see a place like this back in North Carolina. I did some research back then and found a place opening in Charlotte, but nothing was scheduled to come to Raleigh.

Fast forward to my 2nd term as president of our ASHRAE chapter. Topgolf had tried to head to several places in the Triangle area but could not get a location established for several reasons. Another competitor, however, popped up near the PNC Arena where the NC State

Wolfpack basketball team and Carolina Hurricanes play. It was right down the road and called Drive Shack. I saw myself as an average person who enjoyed the mix of socializing and blasting balls on the range in a fun atmosphere. That made this feel like a perfect fit for changing things up with our fall ASHRAE event. Our Triangle board team also knew that Drive Shack was opening soon and would be ready with enough buffer time due to possible delays to make it a good location to host our next fall event.

So here we were, eyeing the option of hosting this event. We had team members on the Research Promotion Committee reach out to do some exploratory review of the facilities, including asking how much it would cost us for the event to be held at their facility. Our previous events were relatively low cost, but we also didn't make as much money as we did in the spring from a sponsorship and registration dollars standpoint. Our chapter back then had an operations budget of about $10,000, based on net revenue from events hosted during the year. I had served on the board in all the officer roles, including Treasurer, so I knew what a typical year looked like financially speaking. We ended each year with the same amount as we started with, so basically called it breaking even.

We reached out to Drive Shack. Our team found out the cost of the event was going to be substantial, to the tune of $7,500 dollars.

I had set one of my management objectives for the Region IV leadership to make money on this fall event. It would be the first of its kind. This was risky. To make this even more challenging, we had to pay 50% of the money up front and the final 50% within five days of the event.

This would mean we were possibly putting 75% of our operations budget on the line for this event.

To hit a number like this, our ASHRAE team needed to generate an attendance of 100+ people for an event that was the first of its kind in the Raleigh area. I could sense a little bit of a pause in our Board of Governors meeting in the early part of the year when we found out the cost.

Could we really get this many people to come to an event we had never done before?

An attendance of 100+ people had never happened in our chapter's history for a fall event based on information older members on our team shared. But something was different with my mind at this moment. Bravery really kicked in while I was digesting all this information to decide what we should do.

We were looking at the best way to fund this event from a cash flow perspective. My belief this event would pay off never wavered, even for a moment. My focus in working with our team was to develop a strategy of action to resolve the cash flow issues and give us a calculated risk that would put us in the best position to win. Then we had to communicate this value to the potential sponsors and get buzz interest in a brand-new event, building a strong connection. Remember in the beginning how I mentioned the Action + Connection concepts being put together to have a major impact on others? This is how it works.

Then, one of our board members and longtime supporter of our chapter did something that I will never forget.

He volunteered to put the $3750 dollars needed for the deposit on his personal credit card.

We had thirty days to pay him back. He used the purchase to get some free vacation miles for his family. It was the perfect win-win scenario, provided we could deliver on our end as a team for this event. My energy was up, seeing this person make this kind of commitment for our team. I know many would not have risked putting this on their personal credit card.

So here I was, along with our research team, calling everyone we knew under the sun to encourage attendance at this event with about two months to go. We promoted the heck out of this event. There was already a lot of buzz about Drive Shack to begin with, being the first place of its kind in Raleigh. We got a steady stream of event registrations very close to the thirty-day cutoff window. Enough money was made to pay our generous person back with the seed money.

Now we were in the final thirty days of the event and our team was in an all-out blitz to reach out and get support for this event to make the final 50% payment. We had someone in our chapter able to pay for the potential losses on this as a backup plan, but I went back to my objectives on this event. We were not going to lose money. I was going to make sure our team was successful in hitting this major accomplishment near our grasp by any means necessary.

I continuously and relentlessly made calls promoting the value of this brand-new event while celebrating the bravery we showed by taking a risk of this magnitude. The registrations kept pouring in during those final thirty days. In the week leading up to the event, we broke even, with $7500 in participant money! But the goal was to make money.

In the final 24-48 hours, even more registrations came in and our event yielded a profit. This was unbelievable for a first-time event with such high risk! Or was it?

While my focus on the event was getting people to attend the event, it was also important to make sure we delivered on all the hype. During the two-month campaign leading up to the event, we communicated our exciting plans for the day to get more registrations. Our research team did an outstanding job getting all the prep work ready as we closed in on our big day.

I remember driving up to this new facility, wondering how all these people attending the event would feel and react. Our team was perfectly organized, making everything easy for people who came to our fundraiser. The Drive Shack team was first class, doing all the onsite prep work. Then the flood of people came in the door, and it was immediately apparent how much impact this event had on all our attendees. There were tons of people blasting golf balls on the range, enjoying the buffet setup, and socializing with each other, having a wonderful time together.

My effort to connect was just as important as the strategy leading up to the successful attendance numbers at the event. I went by each bay to spend a few minutes personally thanking each of the groups that brought people to the event. I also asked for feedback about how things were going or anything we could have done to make this first-time event something better for everyone who attended. I saw people coming to this event who were former members and presidents of the board who had not come to anything in a very long time. It was honestly fun just sitting back and watching all the people coming in having a great time and seeing the impact of my efforts to develop into my best self and lead the team. I didn't really swing a lot of balls or eat much, due to my focus on making sure everyone who came had a great time. One of the former past presidents said something that I will never forget toward the end of that day, which is paraphrased below:

"Kirby, this is the most fun ASHRAE event we have had in a very long time. You and the team did an outstanding job making this experience something memorable for me. The chapter is really in good hands under you and I'm looking forward to seeing how the rest of the year goes."

The Drive Shack did everything I could have imagined, and our entire team won with 105 people attending this fundraiser for ASHRAE research.

We made money at the event. Our calculated risk based on perfect execution (action) led to putting us in a position to draw people to want to be part of this brand-new event (connect). This event permanently altered my mindset and was a shining example of how bravery can be built. I can tell you right now this could have never happened without my newly built self or without a once in a lifetime Triangle Chapter ASHRAE team that deserves to be celebrated for years to come. To put this in historical perspective, we have hosted a fall event at Drive Shack every year since 2019 with very high attendance numbers like the first time during my term as President.

What I learned during this phase of my journey developing bravery was to always bet on and back myself to win, which would lead to big results.

And now it's time to head into the back half of the lion attribute development, focusing on leadership, with another great story to tell of our legendary hall of fame ASHRAE Triangle Chapter team under my two terms as President.

Chapter 15

Leadership Development & Strategy

The first three steps of this system focused on facing your fears, working to grow as an individual, and then taking major risks with no hesitation to put you in a position to focus on the leadership attribute. The back stretch of the lion attributes system was created to help you harness your ability as connector while taking action that came out of the courage, strength, and bravery integration.

As an AEC professional seeking to improve your leadership skills, you've likely noticed that there are numerous books and entire billion-dollar industries that provide only general cookie cutter theories about leadership development. Unfortunately, there are several major flaws with leadership development right now.

- We don't teach leadership skills to technical professionals and assume being a high-ranking individual contributor will make a great leader.
- We hire outside consultants that have no industry experience to show us how to be a leader in the AEC industry.
- We are given general theory that is identically cast across multiple industries but no way to apply it in practice and application to the AEC industry.

The Harvard Business Review reports we spend $200 billion per year on leadership development programs. Studies show that barely 10% of the material is useful, valuable, effective, or applicable. No wonder we have problems with poor leadership in the AEC industry.

> **That means $180 billion per year is wasted on leadership development programs that are ineffective, not applicable, or unable to impact the people they serve.**

Leadership in the AEC industry is more than just a general theory that applies to everyone. The AEC industry is blue collar and has a mindset that is different from everyone else's. This is why leadership development needs to be reinvented. The Lion Attitude exists to change this mentality.

There are so many different versions of what people believe their perfect leader looks like. But one thing is consistent about all leaders: they get better by putting in the work to develop skill sets for connecting with others to create impact. Great leaders are always working on honing their skills and finding new insights daily.

Leadership building is about taking the initiative to lead a group in a way that impacts the team or even those beyond the core members. This is also an area where a major trap can take place. It's the downfall of those who try to get better with leadership attributes by only focusing on their individual skills. Someone I ran across gave an interesting name for this type of behavior, but I am going to keep this clean by calling it "super contributor."

Super contributors are basically larger-sized versions of an individual's previous self before beginning a leadership role. Their focus is too much on themselves and not on the growth and development of the group they are leading. The worst form of the super contributor is a micromanager. This causes team suffering because of this individual's super-sized skills.

It's interesting to look at how this plays out in the sports world. There are a lot of all-time great Hall of Fame players who people would assume should automatically be excellent head coaches or front office executives.

If you look at winning head coaches in the NFL, or any other leagues, there is something unique about most of them:

Most championship winning coaches are usually not Hall of Fame players.

The goal of this section isn't to immediately turn you into a Hall of Fame leader, running an organization on the first day. Leadership is built over time. The big fallacy out there is the belief that holding a management role is a requirement for leading people in business. There are great leaders who are not necessarily the CEOs of Fortune 500 companies, something most in society picture when they hear the term leadership.

What this section focuses on is simply taking the initiative to leading others with your skills. This passion to teach, coach, and guide others is where your ability to learn how to connect really gets harnessed.

Remember in the introduction of Phase Three where I mentioned that lions are elite at Action + Connection at the same time?

You are ready for this challenge now, having developed a strong purpose while setting a daily intention and practice to get better every morning.

You can lead people daily by doing the following things without the need for some fancy title:

- Teaching your Child How to Ride a Bike
- Running a Non-Profit in a Volunteer Position
- Presenting to a Group on a Subject you have Researched
- Taking on a Project with a Team within your Company

As you put in the hard work to build a skill set for connecting with others, you will see something magical happening over time. Suddenly you will notice that people will want to follow you and be a part of what you are working on. They want to be part of the journey. This is a powerful moment, when you realize how important the ability to connect is for impacting others. But what's different in being an effective leader versus adopting the super contributor mindset is you're focusing on working with others and not just your personal development. It takes a lot of patience and time to learn how to lead people, but it's worth it in the long run.

You will also notice changes in how you are perceived as you work on this attribute. People who are focused on others are attractive leaders. Consider the questions below as you delve into this section of development:

Who does a team turn to when things are hard?
Who do they ask for guidance?
How does this person change the team for the better because of their actions and decisions?
Does this person have a plan and strategy?
Can this person connect and build relationships aligned on a common goal together?
Who uplifts the morale of the group?

I'd like to close out this section, before sharing my story of leadership, with something I heard that helped me focus on this attribute:

**People don't follow titles;
they follow great leaders!**

Now let's walk through my journey with my unforgettable example of leadership.

Application Example: Kirby's Unexpected Year as President of the Triangle ASHRAE Chapter – February 2019 to June 2019

One of the interesting things about my experience with the leadership attribute is I learned you never know when an opportunity might come along.

When I joined the Triangle ASHRAE team, I realized I could achieve exponential growth in my leadership journey if I worked with intention while volunteering for roles on the board. I started in 2016 with a plan to serve in each of the officer roles, including Secretary, Treasurer, Vice President & Programs Chair, and President. When I joined ASHRAE and became a part of the leadership team, I was told there was a four-year process for moving my way through the roles toward serving as President. Looking at this from a growth perspective, those 2 ½ years I spent on the board before being thrust into the President's role of our chapter was a good thing. No, I didn't get the standard four-year education, but I was glad to have some chapter leadership experience in various roles as Secretary, Treasurer, and Vice President to draw from.

I remember the first time I saw someone winning our highest national award, what we called for short "The Rudy." I was at my first Chapter Regional Conference in Atlanta, GA, at the Lake Lanier Islands. There was a lot to take in at the conference. The outgoing past President on the Triangle ASHRAE team was working for Wake County Government. I saw how much work he'd put in all year long from a distance because someone at my engineering firm was a member of the Triangle Board of Governors. The level of energy I felt that weekend, seeing all the people celebrating the Triangle team and their accomplishments, plus those of the other six chapters in North Carolina, South Carolina and Georgia, was something that stuck with me.

The Rudy is a massive trophy that was established in 1981. It has the names etched on it of every chapter that has won the award since it was created. This item looks so big, I think of the Stanley Cup every time I get to see it at a conference, or more frequently, when someone wins it locally. Presidents who led their teams to winning this award will tell you all kinds of stories of things that happened during their year leading to the win. I have also heard stories of people who were legit crying over winning this award. So clearly, my first impression was that winning this trophy was a big deal.

ASHRAE chapters focus on growing membership and having an impact on their communities. The award focuses on the areas listed below as part of the winning criteria each year. Chapters get credit for the work they do in each area and are awarded points during the year for specific accomplishments. Running a chapter is very similar to running a business, which is one of the experience areas I was seeking to benefit from as part of the Triangle ASHRAE team. What better way to learn leadership skills than by taking time to volunteer to help others while growing my skills at the same time?

These are the areas ASHRAE judges consider when choosing The Rudy winner:

- Chapter Operations
- Chapter Technology Transfer (CTTC – Called Programs)
- Government Affairs
- Young Engineers in ASHRAE (YEA – Below thirty-five years of age)

- Communications
- Membership Promotion
- Research Promotion
- History

At the end of the year, the Regional Director reviews all the criteria to see which team is the overall winner. The President of this team is awarded a plaque with their name on it. The winning chapter gets their nameplate on the trophy, then gets to take this huge trophy home for the year to celebrate this with their local membership.

My story starts during my Vice President year. I was working under the President elected in 2018. To give some historical context, for four years in a row during my years as Secretary and Treasurer, our chapter won The Rudy. It felt like something special was happening with our Triangle team. During the year I served as Vice President, things went in a direction no one could see coming.

The energy was sky high coming into 2018. We started off the year very out of sync. The current President had gone through some major medical issues during the previous year, so our team knew we needed to be prepared to step up if something happened. As we started off the year, the communication wasn't there between the team and our President.

The President was having more major health issues. Consequently, I, as Vice President, and others on our team, had to take a more active role running the organization during the first half of the year. This led to some major strain for some of our team members, including me, as individuals took on multiple roles. Setting up each meeting felt like a mad scramble. Our President was still trying to be active while dealing with these medical issues.

We went into many meetings and chapter events wondering if our President would be able to make it. He wasn't communicating with us about his status and availability. Keep in mind, ASHRAE is a volunteer organization, so we needed to be respectful of his medical situation. This was someone donating their time while facing serious health issues.

Before implementing a new fall fundraising approach for ASHRAE, we had our final 5k fun run in 2018. This was a breaking point and a low moment for our group. Not only did the President not show up for the event, but our team wasn't getting any communication on what was happening so we could plan for a backup if he could not make it. I remember some of our board members basically reaching out to me and just saying, "Well, Kirby, guess we can mail in our Rudy entry this year rather than attend the ceremonies, and maybe win The Rudy under you next time."

Running that team in crisis mode for six months was not what I'd envisioned. In December of that year, the board needed to get a gauge on the President to see where his head was at. I remember thinking we might be asking him to step aside at this meeting so he could focus on his health and the chapter board team could focus on getting things back on track for the rest of the year. Our fiscal year runs from July to June.

The meeting was very awkward. The President was adamant about staying on in his leadership position running the chapter. I thought, going into this, we might be voting him out, but after hearing him say how committed he was to the rest of the year, that thought went away. We agreed to have more regular communication and I tried to check in specifically to see how I could help him in a support role.

The back half of the year started in 2019. We were preparing for a major event with a 50th anniversary celebration of the Triangle Chapter. Our plan was to invite every living person who was President of the chapter to come and celebrate the history of all the teams over the years. Once again, communication issues occurred in January and February. However, the tension was a lot higher now. You could really feel the strain it was having on the whole team, trying to run an organization with no leadership. The President was still not showing up for events and morale was declining with not only the board and me, but also across the entire membership.

Then the 50th anniversary meeting in February 2019 took place. We had our board meeting before the chapter celebration event. Our team was doing everything it could during this occasion, despite all the internal issues we were having. The President showed up to the meeting and wanted to say a few words before we started. His words were few; he told our team he was stepping down immediately. This resulted in my role being elevated to President of the chapter, on the spot.

Up until this point, our chapter leadership was not living up to what our Triangle team was capable of during the previous years I was on the board. That whole February meeting was a blur, honestly, but it was a relief for our team after eight months of uncertainty and instability. I remember our team rallying around that moment to make the board meeting and the 50th anniversary celebration something fun.

How would our team respond at this point with me running the chapter?

I had been on the team as an individual contributor, but this was the first time I'd be leading a team in this type of role. Something was happening inside me before that moment when my reinvention took place. During the summer of that year, I had been reflecting on my transformation and drew from that to write the following words that evening after the 50th celebration event:

"This team is still capable of winning The Rudy this year. We should not give up on this year without a fight to the very end. Let's go out this year with our heads up high, proud of the efforts we make between now and June 30th."

Our team and board leadership started to work with me specifically to plan how we could rebuild the rest of the year. Keep in mind that my role as Vice President also meant running the programs and setting up meetings that are typically part of the Triangle Chapter member benefits. My goal was to work on setting up the remaining meetings as quickly as possible so I could serve more as an overseer of our chapter, helping others as needed for the remainder of the fiscal year.

The first thing I drew on was my ability to connect. It took a lot of effort to connect all our board members in ways that were not happening in the previous months. This included improving team relationships, which seemed to make our meetings and events significantly better. Many were empathetic as I unexpectedly jumped in to run the chapter. I didn't know what to expect.

As we got to the end of the year, there was a Regional Planning session in Colombia, SC, that included training. Going into things, I started to get a glimpse of how our team's performance was stacking up to others that year. Surprisingly, I found out we seemed to be leading in a lot of areas, which was a sign we had a chance to win The Rudy, despite all the major issues we faced early in the year. I remember sharing at that regional meeting I thought we had a chance to win, which got some puzzled looks, given the disarray we were in.

We closed out the year, then had our next Chapter Regional Conference in Charlotte in September. This was a critical juncture for me, since I had been working on my personal reinvention from scratch during prior months. I felt different going into this conference and knew we had done everything possible to finish strong the previous year. All I could think was if we didn't win, we could look back at seven months of internal issues as the reason for us coming up short.

Our team won some major awards that year in a lot of categories. We were all excited about the Saturday event where The Rudy award would be announced. The moment of truth popped up on the screen and, honestly, I was stunned yet bursting with energy when I saw it:

Rudy Ferguson – Triangle Chapter (Kirby Lee)

The feeling of being able to lead a team to victory under those circumstances of the 2019-2020 year, then staying on as President for another full term, was gratifying. This moment, though, of being awarded this honor despite so many chapter challenges, was where my leadership journey really started. I understood the importance of serving others. It was not perfect or sexy looking, but all the effort put in was what mattered in my growth.

I still had a lot to learn about leadership. This book would have been helpful for me as someone who was very technical, trying to understand how to apply soft skills. This is why working on your leadership with others is one of the five important attributes in developing as a professional.

And we are down to the final lion attribute in Phase Three, which is heart.

Chapter 16

Heart Development & Strategy

Now let's explore the final of the five lion attributes that are part of the integration. It's appropriate we're covering the heart area of the journey at the end of this process. The words I've chosen and the sequence for introducing the five attributes are intentional. Note that the overall theme of Phase Three is focused on teaching you how Action + Connection builds on the first two phases in your professional development. Courage, strength, and bravery are action attributes. Purpose, intention, and motivation are the roots built in Phase One and Two. Leadership and heart deal with the connection area of your development. These are also important in terms of building relationships, self-mastery, and learning how to focus on attaching value to strategies that involve building success stories with others.

Heart is the area that I would say is the toughest of all five attributes in your development journey. When you think of how your heart works, it's a very difficult thing to measure progress on.

How do you know you have a heart to begin with?
Can you see your heart to know if everything is going okay?
Your heart is very much like the HVAC system in your house. When it's not working, everyone around you knows. It impacts your ability to be your best self.

The key component of developing the heart attribute is to focus on connection.

Imagine you are listening to a speech where you see someone really pouring it all out there with fire and passion about a certain subject. That passion is something that is not a measurable thing in terms of some technical tool. What is measurable is the impact it creates. Les Brown did a speech called "Face Your Fears," where he gets to a section of the description of how things feel inside you. Nearly every time that I hear this Les Brown speech, a lot of tears form in my eyes.

But why would a simple audio speech I have heard countless times have this type of impact?

I felt this message and it resonated deeply in my heart; I was feeling the connection.

Les Brown's speaking style had an impact on me that's hard to describe, but it's affected my life in a significant way. His message was the reason I wanted to get out of debt and earn financial freedom. Anyone can listen to his message. Why didn't everyone else feel the same impact that I did? The reason is the connection and heart didn't create the same impact for someone else as it did for me.

If Les Brown didn't have purpose and intention behind his speech, would it have created the same impact?

No. Les Brown needed to have all five lion attributes as well as the ability to get stronger as a speaker, face his fears, take big risks, and put himself in a position to lead people. Finally, Les needed to be able to connect with people's hearts in how he presented to his audience. And this is how Les Brown ended up growing his skills as a professional and a leader, speaking to audiences and major companies all over the world.

There are lots of different ways to connect with people through their heart that can create measurable impact. Great examples of this usually focus on the soft skills realm. A few items that come to mind include:

- Public Speaking to an Audience (or presenting)
- Writing on Social Media about your Experiences (LinkedIn is great example)
- Building New Relationships with People
- Attending Networking Events in your Field of Interest

But the one I plan on touching on in my story is how I learned to connect with my heart through something deeply personal that changed my life:

Learning Emotional Intelligence (EQ) from Ground Zero

Now let's go forward on to the final leg of Phase Three, sharing how this subject changed my entire life permanently.

Application Example: Kirby's Discovery & Development of Emotional Intelligence from Ground Zero.

The words still ring from the darkest days of my time working for the government, words spoken by a department employee in November 2019:

"Kirby, you have no emotional intelligence."

I had been undergoing a major transformation in the summer of 2019. My purpose was unbreakable during that moment. I was in the early stages of going through the Morning Start-Up and starting to realize how important it was to focus daily on myself. Doing so was having an impact on the direction I wanted to travel in life professionally.

I was intentional about my focus on building soft skills along with relationships to help me learn how to better connect with others. Many times, my skills felt sharp, but there were other times when I sensed something was missing as I tried to communicate with people. When I first started learning how to interact with people in 2013, I studied a book about reading personalities by Dr. Tony Alessandra called *The Platinum Rule*.

This book provided a common sense, easy to understand version of the Myers Briggs analysis. He broke it down into four quadrants: Director, Thinker, Socializer, and Relator.

I took his test and discovered I was a solid Director. I spent years trying to master and understand every aspect of my own personality, plus learn how to communicate with other personalities to build relationships. It took a lot of work. I remember some in leadership roles at engineering firms didn't appreciate the time I was putting into learning how to develop this skill.

Five years later, when I was working for the government under the person who hired me, it felt like I had mastered this skill, feeling good about how I was building relationships. Hearing someone say I had no emotional intelligence after working to rebuild myself from scratch for months really hit me hard. Why was I still having issues building relationships after all this work?

There was a class put on by someone in my department about Emotional Intelligence. I decided to take it. Prep work required included reading *Emotional Intelligence (EQ) 2.0* by Travis Bradberry and Jean Graves, and doing a self-assessment of my EQ score before attending. Thanksgiving break was coming up. We were going to be doing some traveling to see my wife's family in Pennsylvania with our toddler daughter in tow.

Little did I know this Thanksgiving would be a weekend that would completely change the trajectory of my life.

To give some general background of emotional intelligence, there are four focus areas that make up EQ. Self-awareness and self-management are the first two areas covered. These focus on doing the inner work to first manage, then master your emotions. The second half focuses on social awareness and relationship management, with work toward reading the emotions of others in concert with using your own to build successful relationships. This book did a very good job of providing general strategies in each area, plus explaining how the impact of EQ was something that could be improved with effort. There is a lot of data that ties higher EQ with promotions and making more money in life, compared to those with lower EQ.

As I was reading the initial part of this book, I was starting to realize something important:

The ability to connect was just as important as being able to act.

I also started to realize that developing my ability to connect would help me create more value to teams and a bigger impact on others around me. I was already strong with my ability to act at this stage, but looking back, this alone was not enough to be the type of leader I sought to be in the future for others. I needed to change how I chose to act to be able to master the heart part of the journey. And then it hit me while in the hotel room reading about emotional intelligence as I prepared for this class:

"Kirby, use your ability with action to learn how to connect. Do not turn into an attacker!"

That weekend, while in Pennsylvania, I discussed my book topics with my father-in-law, asking him questions about his experience. He was a volunteer firefighter and chief of the department in his local town for a very long time before his retirement. He seemed to have a really good idea of how to build relationships with people. I remember him telling me stories about how he was learning to connect as well, and how his approach was very similar to mine as an attacker. We had talked about things before, but something was different this time.

As I was sharing material from *Emotional Intelligence (EQ) 2.0* for the first time, I was starting to really question everything I had done to develop my soft skills and leadership strategies up to this point. Clearly, I had been missing something, but I could not put my finger on what had been negatively affecting my relationships for years. The book and my father-in-law helped me understand the missing piece. He explained to me that mastering how to read personalities was a key part of my journey up to this point. But the next level was being aware of my own emotions while reading others at the same time. Learning how to do this would enable me to connect with people in a way I had never done before.

The first thing I started to think about was how this resembled aiming at an archery target several hundred yards away. On a normal day, if you aimed at the target exactly the same way each time, you would, in theory, get the same result. However, there are little micro shifts in your body and mind, plus external factors like the wind, which go into calculations for hitting a target. Failing to read those shifts could result in being one or two degrees off in accuracy. But over the distance, this small difference could result in missing the target by a wide margin. This was a breakthrough. Suddenly it made sense as to why my communication was off and why I was having trouble with relationships.

My focus needed to be on reading personalities AND emotions at the same time!!!

What I realized in that moment was when in a non-emotional state, I was effective at building relationships and connecting with others. But when emotions factored into the equation, I failed to make those adjustments or catch the micro shifts. Suddenly, a communication would go sideways because I didn't read the emotional intelligence component and associated shift taking place.

But how was I going to learn a skill that wasn't really a straightforward task, like writing a technical book?

The foundation of this book is built on my version of emotional intelligence growth. Phase One is designed to help you identify and develop your purpose to begin the process of personal and professional growth. Phase Two involves integrating reading into your Morning Start Up routine and learning how to apply it daily. Phase Three provides ideas on how you can connect with people through the heart attribute by applying strategic effort with Action + Connection.

My journey with EQ focused on the self-awareness and management areas, since this would improve my skills in social awareness and relationship management. When I got back from Pennsylvania, I reached out to my mom and dad, along with other trusted family members, to have deep and open conversations about how I made others feel when I communicated with them. My family unanimously shared I was an attacker who didn't know how to connect.

From there, I started to think deeply about my emotions to try to understand all the aspects of what I was feeling. My EQ journey goal was to be able to master my own emotions, then be able to use this mastery to read others for better overall relationships. The first 2-3 months were hard. I found myself paralyzed as I tried to pause every time I felt an emotion to get a deeper understanding of what it meant. During those tough times, I would reach out to someone I trusted. The conversation was always centered around trying to understand why I experienced these emotions when I did. I started to learn that when I couldn't read or acknowledge those emotions, they would come out in different ways.

A few weeks later, I attended an all-day class to discuss the EQ book material. I was surprised to see someone who warmed my heart. The trainer of my prior class on the Covey *7 Habits of Highly Effective People* concept was the instructor for the emotional intelligence class too. During this class, we went through the impact of Covey's teachings, which focused on leadership development.

This Covey class changed my life by helping me find me. I was so happy to see the trainer and enjoyed getting to share my stories of growth since that three-day-long June 2019 session. What stood out as most beneficial in this class was having a partner to be vulnerable with during the journey.

I could not find a single person from my workplace who wanted to be my partner in applying the EQ workshop principles. That was likely because no one attending from the government department group put effort into applying this material as part of their daily practice, except me. So, I took the initiative to work with some people outside of my workplace and check in with the trainer to discuss areas where I could focus.

It took about six months of hard work and daily effort, then suddenly, some magic started to happen. I was getting compliments on how I was building relationships with others and feeling a level of connection that I never had before. My work on myself was paying off. I could even feel the emotions coming without letting them consume me anymore. Even more interesting was that I could now start to clearly articulate how I was feeling in a way that didn't damage relationships.

I still focus on EQ daily. While I am not perfect by any means, this intentional effort backed up by my purpose created the impact I wanted from a leadership perspective. The goal behind developing the heart attribute is to master the ability to connect with others. Each time you make an intentional effort with purpose to build something meaningful through connecting with others, it results in a lasting impact beyond just that moment in time.

You have worked hard to this point, trying to develop all five lion attributes, building a lot of strong roots in leadership. The final leg of the journey puts the entire system together with the closing stage of Phase Four.

It's time to lock in on some targets to hunt and create an accountability support system so you can apply what we've been working on in practice. This will help keep you going so you can develop leadership skills that create impact for a lifetime.

Phase 4

Lion Targets
& Pride Support

We're getting near the end of a valuable process and journey. It's time to explore what the final leg of your destination will look like. If you have done all the work in the first three phases of this book, you should feel like a completely different person professionally. Others should be starting to see this due to the leadership skills you've developed.

Phase One was focused on a tear down and a reinvention of yourself from scratch, based on Intention + Motivation to build a strong purpose from within. Phase Two put more of a daily focus on your efforts to strengthen and harness the power of your purpose with the Morning Start Up. This is designed to help you improve at a micro level with daily, consistent practice to keep your purpose strong. In Phase Three, you turned loose this new purpose and self-development to be tested in the five lion attributes. Here we worked on how to integrate them as you continue to build your skills to Act + Connect at the same time.

Phase Four puts everything together to set you up for the rest of your life with success, happiness, and fulfillment because of the leadership skills you've developed. This will create value for yourself and everyone around you. You might ask, "Kirby, why didn't you set this up in Phase Three, since I worked on the integration of the attributes here?" Well, the answer is, to hunt prey in the wild like lions do, you must prove that you can deliver results consistently. It's basic logic.

For example, no one would have any chance of being successful in reaching their target if that goal was to run a marathon when prep work didn't include running a single mile. You must prove you are willing to do some very hard work, which includes conditioning yourself over time just to hit that one-mile target. Then, you feel incredible about this accomplishment and are ready to set a bigger goal targeting your end destination.

The aim of this part of the book, based on all the work you've done so far, can be summarized in one word:

Triumph!

The key leadership development concepts in this book build upon each other to create a systematic, methodical, and practical approach. It can be expressed with the following mathematical equation:

Intention + Motivation + Purpose + Action + Connection = Triumph (I+M+P+A+C=T)

If you look at the words, you can see that each of the items in this equation are areas where lions excel daily. Lions put all these traits together better than any other animal in the wild. This is what allows lions to have the I+M+P+A+C=T they do as apex predators. It's why they're called Kings of the Jungle.

Is it any surprise that lions seem to win a lot of battles and get to live a life like no other animal in the wild?

Lions are rare animals for a reason.

If you want to be rare, you must do something rare.

You are now ready to put together some wins and create I+M+P+A+C=T by actively applying the leadership skills you've built inside with an outward focus for the final leg of the journey. This starts with setting your sights on some prey to hunt down.

Chapter 17

Lion Prey Hunting Development & Strategy

I did a lot of research on the impact of setting targets in the five areas focused on in this book as I revisited my self-development journey in 2020. I thought deeply about Phase Four. In this section, I felt it was important to spotlight purpose built from Intention + Motivation (Phase One) and Daily Self-Development (Phase Two) as part of that process.

I'm baffled by the statistics on setting targets:

- Only 3% of the Population Sets Targets for Themselves.
- Only 1% of the Population Actually Writes Them Down.

> **Do you realize that getting to this point of setting meaningful goals makes you better prepared for success than 97% of the population and 99% if you write them down?**

This statement alone should tell you how powerful it is to have the system we've worked on in Phases One to Three of the book installed in your toolbox. Some of the prey you have in your sight should be hard to track down, but you are ready for this hunt. When you think about setting targets, think about these simple words I heard in a speech, "The goal has to challenge you to work toward something meaningful, otherwise there will be no impact."

I set targets in January of 2020 built on the five lion attributes from Phase Three with an overall goal to hit as many of the five as possible by December 31st. My logic was based on results I had already achieved in each of these areas. I used that information to set my first goals for the year. Hitting these targets was possible because I had built up the confidence to do so. My moment of truth took place on December 31, 2019, when I wrote them down on a board where I could always view them.

When we moved into our new house in April of 2020, which was during the height of early pandemic crisis reactions, I took my goals and put them in my brand-new office space. These were posted inside the door so I could see them when I walked in daily. Each month I would look at them and review how things were going. I wanted to see if everything was on track or if adjustments needed to be made to hit my targets.

The five goals in Phase Four are targets that represent the areas covered in Phase Three, namely:

Courage, Strength, Bravery, Leadership, & Heart

It's exciting doing things for the first time while integrating the attributes of the lion into your professional life. Each of those moments in Phase Three should have felt like an energy rush that made you feel powerful. Hitting them should include a big celebration since there is so much growth and expansion that comes from what you must do to reach them.

One of the best ways to set up targets in the five areas mentioned is using the basic SMART format. Let's put this in terms of how lions hunt in the wild.

When a lion sets a target, they have a very *specific* plan of how they want to hunt down an animal in the wild. Lions have a *measurable* way of tracking their progress, assessing how the hunt is going as they zero in on their target. The target must be something the lion is capable of catching (*actionable*). Satisfying hunger makes it *relevant* to the overall purpose of why the lion is hunting to begin with. Since he doesn't want to starve, there's a *timely* duration objective for reaching his target.

If your target meets all these criteria, then you should put your five goals somewhere you can see daily as you visualize your outcomes. The objective is to focus on things in that present moment that will move the needle toward the target you are hunting.

Of course, you can set targets with a shorter duration to get some momentum going. However, I recommend yearly targets since that gives you plenty of time to focus on the possibility of hitting all five targets in a realistic time frame. During some months, you might put major focus on only one or two of the targets, while the other three might be background work, with plans to hit those targets set for later in the year.

During each week I suggest trying to set aside thirty minutes on Sunday evening to look back on your five lion targets. It's a good time to use some of your journaling time in Phase Two to recall what went well, what didn't go well, and how you can keep the momentum going to hit a big target this year.

It's likely you'll experience setbacks as you work toward your targets. Do you really think that everything is going to happen in some perfect step-by-step way to bring you something big you want to hunt down? This is why the foundation steps of Phases One and Two are in place. They're there to help you stay out of spirals that happen when things don't go according to plan.

People with weak purpose or poor self-development will usually give up on big targets. That makes them like most of the population who fail to keep New Year's Resolutions set on January 1ˢᵗ one week later. There are always jokes about how many people head to the gym in January. That becomes a much smaller number in February, since most have given up on their health and fitness goals by then.

I'd like to share how the application of the lion target system worked in practice for me.

Application Example: Kirby's 2023 Year of Lion Targets in Practice

One of the core beliefs of the lion behavior I have been covering in this book is that lions don't announce to prey they are being hunted. They hunt prey in silence, simply working to improve their skills and circumstances as they pursue their targets daily. Announcing your moves all the time would tip off a lion's prey, which will usually result in the target running away.

The goal of this final leg of the journey is to be focused on hitting the targets and not talking about hitting them. These lion traits and behaviors are what make people who adopt the system in this book grow in their professional and leadership development differently than the average person. There is a saying that you can let your results *roar* for you, which is more powerful than anything you can say in words.

I am going to use my life in 2023 as an illustration of how the lion target hunting system looks, so it will be easier to understand how this happens in practice. Since I had already established a strong purpose as described in Phase One, and worked on my self-development daily, I knew the areas I wanted to focus on for the year.

My focus included aiming for the five targets. In a perfect world, people would hit five out of five targets each time, but that is something that should be very hard to do. Most years I usually hit three or four of the five targets on my board.

Courage Target – Write *The Lion Attitude* book.

Strength Target – Lose remaining weight to my final goal of 140 pounds.

Bravery Target – Bring in revenue from additional consulting work matching 75% of what I used to make working for the government.

Leadership Target – Successfully lead the ASHRAE Chapter Regional Conference with positive feedback from society team. Generate a profit from the event and hit the attendance target of 125 people.

Heart Target – Grow following base on LinkedIn to 22,500 as part of the marketing for *The Lion Attitude.*

Here's a quick summary of each of these targets. I also share how they all played out at the end of this section. Notice that some of the targets have time-dependent deadlines to hit. They also have clear measurables and are relevant to my overall purpose. I have kept the goals specific. Based on my research, these were things I believed could be done.

After I developed these targets, I put a whiteboard in my office on December 31st to get ready for the new year. Since I was journaling with my Morning Start Up, I would check in on work progress concerning one or two of these items each day. Note that I was never trying to focus on moving the needle on all five targets at the same time.

Here is where the real world comes into play, since we are not always 100% motivated all the time. There were lulls and periods where I got a little complacent working on these areas. When I hit those episodes, I went back to my purpose and didn't beat myself up because things had stalled. However, I did ask myself some questions during those periods so that flatline achievement was a temporary speed bump. This was important if I wanted to hunt down the target that year.

- Why are you hunting these targets to begin with?
- How will it feel if you hit this target?
- Is this target too challenging in the time allotted? Does it need to be broken down into mini targets?
- What would it feel like if I gave up on this?
- Does the strategy on hunting this target need to be different?
- Does this target align with my overall purpose?

Below is a short summary of how it went trying to capture all the prey that I locked in to hunt down in 2023.

Courage Target – Triumph

I broke down doing all the writing of the draft of this book in monthly increments. However, the leadership goal of guiding our Triangle ASHRAE Chapter conference team was going to consume all summer months. So, my plan was to do as much of the writing as possible, then take May through August off. I would pick up and finish up the writing in the back half of the year.

What I didn't see coming was the editing process. It was something I never could have envisioned when I first started. It was a struggle in the early stages, and I ended up doing a major rewrite of the Introduction and Phase One after I completed the first draft of the book. When I got back to crafting the material for this book after the conference, my writing got better. I also started to get a clearer picture of how this book should flow.

This was a courage target designed to conquer fear. I worried if all this work would create the intended impact I was shooting for within the Architecture/Engineering/Construction community. Facing this fear had a lasting impact on me. It also resulted in many connections and relationships formed along the way. I am grateful to all the people around me who contributed to the strategy, content, and all changes I made while writing this book.

I ended up finishing the draft on the last day of December. This was just in time to switchover into the New Year with new targets. This includes the editing phase, plus the final leg of the creation process.

Strength – Partial Victory

The weight loss journey for me has been quite a long one. This was the year I was going to close out the deal and get to my final overall target set in 2019. I made a lot of progress in the previous years and could see the end in sight.

In the first half of the year, I was complacent about my weight loss and started to gain some of what I lost back. The cold winter months have been difficult for me in North Carolina. I found myself not feeling as inspired to work out. My Morning Start Up routine was breaking down. Most of my weight loss usually happened during the summer when it was warm outside and I could enjoy the breeze and outdoors.

I remember being on a business trip and looking at the scale, seeing that I had gained half the weight I lost back. I felt shame; something just said to go back to my purpose. I questioned how I could let this happen after a nearly three-year journey to get to this final weight loss destination.

In that hotel room, I wrote down why I was complacent and then focused on how I was better than the habits I was allowing into my life that took me off track from my target. I realized the biggest difference leading to my getting off course was that I was traveling a lot more for business and not adjusting for these lifestyle changes.

So, I got back into my Weight Watchers routine and made it a mini goal to get back to the original low weight I was prior to the slide. I was now working and trying to eat better on vacations/trips/ family gatherings for the first time ever. I felt the sacrifices now would result in accomplishments I could carry with me for the rest of my life.

I lost all the weight gained over the summer by October and then some, weighing twenty pounds less than the previous year. I now feel like I'm in the best shape I have ever been.

I didn't hit my end-of-year target but came very close. This is an example that shows that even when I push myself and don't hit the mark, I can still feel proud of the improvements I made from the prior year. You can too.

Guess what my next 2024 Strength Goal will be?

Closing the deal for good on reaching my ideal weight!

Bravery – Partial Victory

For the past several years I have done freelance consulting work. As part of this I've been growing my skills and learning how to focus my leadership achievements on my passion to help others. I believe that if you do enough with your passions, you will create sufficient value and impact to be able to monetize what you offer to others.

I set ambitious targets in previous years for saving extra money, paying off debt faster, and putting aside extra for our daughter's college education down the road. I went into the year seeing my consulting doing well and being able to strike a nice balance between family and my full-time job in regional HVAC equipment sales.

This year I knew it would be a lot harder to hit the targets I set. I was also writing this book, so thought the value generated from consulting and anything related to the book would likely help me now, and also be an investment in my future.

Opportunities in the consulting space dried up toward the back half of the year. Part of this was because my focus was on the book. I had also taken the entire summer off to ensure that the ASHRAE Conference would be successful. I ended up getting about 75% of what I had targeted for freelance income this year. But I did learn a lot about marketing strategies for my consulting business while working on relationships that would put me in a better position for the future.

The book also gives me an opportunity to be in the room to build new relationships during the second half of the year, after it's been published. I plan on resetting this target for the coming year now that I know how to better market myself and have a clearer understanding of all it takes to publish a book. I think I have a great chance to capture this target next year.

Leadership – Triumph

The ASHRAE Chapter Regional Conference, in its final stretch this past year, I was appointed in June of 2021 to lead the conference preparations for 2023. Back then, in the summer of 2021, I, with help of a support team, set only three specific targets for the event:

- Attendance of 125 People with Family-focused Objective
- Event Generated Profit for the Triangle Chapter
- Positive Feedback from all Parties at the Event

This regional conference is an event held once a year and hosted by each chapter every seven years in the Region IV area. The conference includes business meetings, technical sessions for professional development, social events, and awards banquets. This is the one time each year that chapters in North Carolina, South Carolina, and Georgia get together with the Region IV team. The General Chair's role is to get the event ready for all these people to attend.

In 2022 we had done all the planning well in advance, had the hotel booked, and the entire event mapped out. Now it was time to advertise the event to get attendance locked in, work on sponsorships to help offset the event costs, and detail exactly the final arrangements regarding traveling around the site for events.

We held this event in downtown Wilmington, North Carolina, at the Hotel Ballast. It was a perfect venue on the waterfront of the Cape Fear River. Our team of ten volunteers from the Triangle Chapter was able to raise a significant amount of sponsor dollars. Tons of people brought their kids to have fun as a family.

Our team put in a lot of work in the summer of 2023 for this event. Our Region IV leadership was filled with great partners who supported our objectives. Here were the results of this conference:

- 135 people attended.
- The event generated a profit for the chapter.
- We got positive feedback from all involved in the event.

Leading this group was just another stretch for me to grow my leadership skills. I had a different perspective with a more refined and polished Lion Attitude system installed going into this experience versus being President of the Triangle Chapter in 2019-2020. It was also heartwarming seeing so many children coming and playing together during the whole time we held this event. I built a lot of relationships as well that I think will play a part in bigger things for me in the future.

I was proud of this win in August and would happily do this again if it came around in seven more years. Guess we shall see what the future looks like down the road.

Heart – Partial Victory

Two years ago, I realized that I needed to work on my social media presence as part of the preparation for this book. My strategy was to increase my followers by about four times to be ready to launch this book out to the public.

I had never really done any posting, and honestly was just having a great time building a following and telling stories about how I had learned so much in my Lion Attitude journey. It was interesting that daily online writing was helping me craft my message for this book.

What I didn't see coming was the number of relationships I built. I noticed that the more I shared my stories, the more impact I had. Things just took off. My goal behind social media was not to go viral. I simply wanted to figure out how to build my personal brand as part of this book journey.

The people who served as my book beta readers were all people I met on social media. We share a special connection. Nearly every early reader of this book is in the design and construction industries.

I was surprised by how much I overestimated the number of new people who would follow me on social media. The speed at which I built a following in the first year wasn't sustainable for the second. I ended up hitting about half my goal. My focus on socials is to just tell stories, help people, and create an impact for others around me. I feel like I did that, so was happy with the outcomes, even if I didn't hit my numbers.

Recap of Five Lion Targets – 2023

Last year was a great year of growth and expansion. The biggest win was writing this book, hoping to make an impact on leadership within the

Architecture/Engineering/Construction industry. I learned a lot about myself and made a lot of great relationships during the entire year. I also started to learn how to be a better leader by balancing Action + Connection.

I am grateful to have shared this experience with you, the reader, and hope that this system I put together will help you, as a professional, impact others. It's crazy to think this book and the strategy for growth it outlines was originally just me, trying to fix my career and build my leadership skills. If you would have told me five years ago I would write a book about my story and journey, I would have thought you were crazy.

When I add up the wins, I would say I'm looking at a three or four out of five in terms of hitting targets, which is a pretty good year. The best I ever did with the lion targets was 4.5 of five, but maybe I can get better in the future to do my first ever year of hitting five of five targets.

A community and accountability system can help to keep you on track as you build your first year's targets. Let's explore how you can use your lion pride to be a north star for your leadership development.

Chapter 18

Lion Pride Support System, Accountability, Development, & Strategy

In Phase One of this book, we covered how the reinvention process, and as part of this, developing your purpose, is something that comes from within. This must be done alone as you fortify your foundation through Intention + Motivation. What you will notice as you go through the steps and get familiar with the tools covered is people will want to come along with you for the journey.

This is a great thing to do in Phase Four, when it's time to explore the new circle you've formed to find a great accountability and social support system. Bringing others in at this point will serve you well as you work on hunting prey with your five targets each year.

As I was building these phases of the system, it was interesting to hear people in my professional circle making comments like:

"Kirby, you have changed so much. What you have done transforming yourself is incredible. Tell me how you did all this."

"Kirby, you have worked so hard to learn how to connect with others. I can really see that work paying off now."

"Kirby, how did you make all this happen and what did you do? You seem like a completely new person."

Now is the time, in this final stretch, to start really solidifying what I call your lion pride. These are the people you want to be able to talk to privately about how things are going. They're your support system when you need to figure out the best way to move forward when facing roadblocks as you work toward your targets. Lions are social animals. They operate in families, working together, growing the pride so that everyone wins. You have built yourself to this point from the inside out, so you'll start to see people attracted to you who align with the objectives you've set as a leader.

I mentioned earlier that lions never announce to their prey they are being hunted. This is important for you too, so you're able to keep energy focused on getting your target in the early stages of this transformation. This doesn't mean that you, as a newly built lion, will be doing everything alone. You will have to rely on the relationships and lions around you to work together, even when the prey is what you identify to hunt. Keep in mind that lions take the spoils back to the pride so everyone can eat when a hunt is successful.

Your lion pride will generally include four to five people who you feel a strong connection with. This team might take you even further than you are currently envisioning on your leadership journey. Great candidates to help you through your development in Phase Three are strong at Action + Connection. The more you lean into all the work done in this book, the more you will attract these people to you, so don't be concerned if they don't all show up at the same time.

Use your lion pride to help you with accountability and responsibility for the big targets you decide to hunt. I used to cringe when I heard the word "accountable" while working at various places. Typically, at least in my experience, the word was used with some negative connotation and usually as a weapon of fear, warning that if you made a mistake, something bad would happen to you.

We are not using this as a fear tactic, but as a positive force to keep you moving forward into your best version as a leader. If you have learned how to apply everything in this book, you simply take ownership of things that didn't go well and work with your lion pride to find a better way to move forward from a lesson learned.

Below I share my application of the concept. This includes how my lion pride was built, and how I made myself accountable during the year.

Application Example: Kirby's Lion Pride Support System & Accountability

In October, I was really struggling with getting back into the book. I was also still working on social media, trying to build relationships within the Architectural/Engineering/Construction community in preparation for this book launch. As I mentioned, this was a courage target for me this year, and it was starting to feel like I wasn't going to make it.

Someone in my lion pride, who I am close to and really look up to, wrote a book last year. This person is in my pride because she has achieved much higher leadership levels than I have. If I had to guess (I've never worked with her, so don't know), she's likely strong at Action + Connection, which is clearly a powerful combination.

My goal in our first meeting, as I was learning about her background, was to help her. We were both reaching out to those in the design and construction world. She was looking to help people from a different perspective than I was. It seemed like we could collaborate on a project, and I could help her build relationships at the same time.

"Kirby, what you have created is game changing. You need to share this with others. Let's take them on the journey together and share your story out to the world."

Of course, I was thinking, *Lions don't announce targets until they have taken them out.* This was still a core concept I followed, even after we talked. But then I realized she was teaching me something, which really had me thinking. Making more strategic connections by sharing the information privately with her would help in my effort to build a strong lion pride around me.

I connected with four other people on social media who fit the bill for what I sought from those in my support system. I chose to make the effort to build deeper relationships beyond what I had done earlier in the year. I felt a connection to these people and accountable in a way that I had not experienced before.

For the first time, being accountable was not a scary thing that was used as a shadow version of the "blame game." This was something I had seen a lot of in my career. Suddenly, my writing started to flow. Even my editor asked me about my new inspiration.

These relationships helped me attract more people who were aligned with my purpose. My lion pride was with me every step of the way as I worked on this book, offering support, guidance, and strategic ideas I hadn't considered before. When you operate with a strong lion pride, you can do just about anything you wish, in both your profession and personal life. Lions always protect their pride.

My lion pride is responsible for this book developing the way it did. Each of these strong lions and lionesses pushed me further, encouraging me to be accountable. They helped me get to my ultimate target of delivering this book, and hopefully having an impact on you as the reader. I am grateful beyond words for everything they did professionally for me as a leader, but also as personal friends. They will always be part of my lion pride, connected for life because of the impact they had on me!

Being accountable about hunting your targets by having a lion pride support system will be the reason you keep going in the right direction as a leader.

Wrap Up and Conclusions

First off, I want to thank you and express my gratitude for you taking this book in your hands and reading it through to the final pages. You have gone through a long journey. When I started building my Lion Attitude, I didn't yet have the tools to develop my leadership skills as a technical professional in the design and construction industry.

My goal was to build them with a simple approach in a process-oriented way, based on a strong purpose, so a technical professional in our industry like you could understand my approach. I also wanted to provide real world examples of what success looks like in each section to make it easier for you to apply these concepts to create a significant impact in your life.

Phase One was designed to rebuild yourself with purpose, which is usually a critical missing component for most technical professionals seeking leadership roles. We built a system and process so you could find your purpose based on Intention + Motivation. Purpose is not something someone can hand to you. You must get this part, get to this place, on your own. Then you brand and embody this purpose, making it strong enough to stand up to challenges that will come up in the future. And finally, in this phase, we explored how to realign your vision and make changes to become the future self you want to be.

Phase Two put emphasis on developing daily habits in the morning, creating a micro-level focus on strengthening your purpose with even higher levels of Intention + Motivation. We explored strategies for the six areas of the Morning Start Up: Reading, Gratitude, Exercise, Journaling, Meditation, and the 5AM Club. Adding these to your mornings will create more present-focused days and allow you to really take your purpose to a higher level.

The big tests came for your purpose in Phase Three, with the lion attribute integration of all the skills of Action + Connection. You took action to face your fears with courage, got to work on being stronger, and took large risks with bravery. Then we explored tools to grow your professional skills by working on your ability to connect with leadership and heart. At the end of this process, your mind should be focused on Act + Connect and not just one item at a time. Remember, the attacker and con artist aren't good examples of leadership.

Once you've proven yourself in Phase Three, it's time to move forward, hunting and chasing lion targets in Phase Four. Here you worked on developing a lion pride support system to form a group you can be accountable to for hitting your targets. This is not an ending journey after the first year, as you would expect. There is still room for growth and expansion every single year, to learn new things and become the best leadership version of yourself so you can effectively serve others.

Now you are ready to go forth on your journey to share the impact of the Lion Attitude. I wish you the best on your journey.

I leave you with the math equation again that covers each trait the lion possesses as an apex predator. I believe developing these skills will make you successful as a professional and a leader. If you devote yourself to all the steps in this book, you will be able to create I+M+P+A+C=T for the rest of your days using the system. I give you my word on this!

Intention + Motivation + Purpose + Action + Connection = Triumph (I+M+P+A+C=T)

This isn't goodbye for us. It is now time for your journey to begin. Your path will be different from my own. On your road under construction, I will be coming along with you, cheering you every step of the way, and celebrating your triumphs.

I've prepared a toolkit that includes all the resources that were invaluable in my own leadership reinvention as a special gift to help you. My contact information is also provided so you can reach out if you need further assistance on your journey toward living your professional life like a lion in the AEC industry.

Acknowledgements

This book would not have been possible without the many people in the AEC industry who have believed in me and my purpose to make an IMPACT on current and future leaders. I want to express my eternal gratitude to the following people, including my family, friends, colleagues, supporters, and the beta reader team for helping make this dream a reality.

To my wife Tara and daughter Maddie: You are at the front and center as the top-level foundational members of my lion pride. You have watched me completely change as a result of The Lion Attitude in every aspect of my life. I am grateful this system has made me a better husband, father, and leader for our family. I wouldn't be where I am today without your support.

To Chris Ross: Your speeches on Fearless Motivation inspired me to write this book. You are with me every day as I listen to your speeches. Your words have guided my steps for the past five years and will continue to do so.

A special thanks to Michelle Pecak: We connected over a year ago as AEC professionals at a point in both our lives where it made sense for us to take a journey together. Many of the critical components of this leadership system would not have been possible without you. Just think, a simple conversation in December created the I+M+P+A+C=T formula, the Act + Connect, and many key concepts this book was built on. I will always consider you one of my greatest partners and am proud of what we've accomplished in our effort to reinvent the AEC community.

To Dr. Colleen Saringer: You are one the greatest people I have ever met on this earth. I knew the first day we spoke that we would be walking on many journeys together. *The Lion Attitude* would not have been possible without you. I've also appreciated your partnership on everything else we've worked on together. My dream of earning the right to celebrate doing the Debt Scream in Nashville, TN. would not have been possible without you.

To Eugina Jordan: My journey through writing on LinkedIn put us together. I have never met a more inspirational person than you. You make me a better leader. It all started with the words "Kirby, you should take all these people on the journey with you….."

To Norm Brautigam: You are the greatest leader I have ever been around in my professional career. Your ability and mastery of Act + Connect with others is something I work every day to model so I can make the same I+M+P+A+C=T on others as you have on me. I will always consider you my mentor and trusted advisor.

To my beta readers (Jeff Johnson, Melissa Cohen, Michelle Pecak, Sharon Rusk, Abby Massey, Erika Rothenberger, Allisa Randall, and Ann Moran): Thank you for being part of my life. You have impacted me in many different ways. None of the dreams of how I wanted to I+M+P+A+C=T others would have been possible without your support in making this a better book.

To my editor, Nanette Levin, and my publishing and launch mentor, Diana Needham: Thank you for coming on this journey with me to make this once in a lifetime dream come true. It's crazy to look back and realize that this all started with a networking conversation in March 2021. We have had a lot of highs and some setbacks along the way, but we made it to the finish line together. I am grateful that you came along and walked this very long path to make this vision a reality.

There have been many people who have followed this journey on LinkedIn from the beginning. It's a very long list. I want to express my gratitude for all the support you have provided along with the positive I+M+P+A+C=T you've made on me.

I talk a lot in the beginning and end of the book about the importance of the lion pride in leadership. I have found my pride members, and they are now with me for life.

To the readers of this book: I hope you will take this system and go out to make an I+M+P+A+C=T in the AEC industry. Let's keep up the good work so we can have a place where all the talent in the world recognizes this is one of the most rewarding fields of all professions.

Thank you, with more gratitude than you know.

Kirby

About The Author

 Holding a bachelor's degree in mechanical engineering, Kirby Lee has twenty-three years of direct experience in every facet of the Architecture/Engineering/Construction (AEC) industry. He's a 3rd generation HVAC construction business professional.

Kirby is a registered Professional Engineer in the State of North Carolina. He also holds certifications as a LEED Accredited Professional in Building Design + Construction, Certified Energy Manager, Certified Energy Auditor, and Green Building Engineer. Kirby has also worked in numerous roles, including leadership positions in consulting engineering, owner's representative, and HVAC equipment sales within the AEC sector.

During his time working in AEC sales, Kirby led and trained salespeople in fifteen different states. He's also helped develop engineering staff in the Raleigh, NC market. Much of his leadership insight has come from studying best practices and implementing them into his life over a five-year period. His book highlights the system he created to help address the shortcomings in leadership development in the AEC industry.

In addition to holding leadership roles at several engineering firms, Kirby is an active volunteer in the industry. He has held key leadership roles within the Triangle Chapter of ASHRAE (American Society of Heating Refrigeration and Air Conditioning Engineers), including serving as President for two terms. He also assumed the role of Region IV Conference Chair for 2023. In these chapter and regional roles, he led teams that performed with record metrics at both the chapter and conference levels.

Based on his direct hands-on experience in the AEC industry, Kirby realized that the current leadership development programs were significantly flawed. He set out to reinvent leadership training principles to ensure current and future generations of AEC leaders could develop the leadership skills required in this evolving industry. This resulted in his specialized leadership development system tailored specifically to the AEC industry, an industry he has loved for his entire life.

To learn more about the Lion Attitude services and offerings, visit www.LionAttitude.com.

Connect with Kirby on LinkedIn at:
www.linkedin.com/in/kirby-lee-lionattitude
or email him directly at Kirby@LionAttitude.com.

Your Bonus Gift – The Lion Attitude Toolkit

Thank you for joining me in the mission of reinventing leadership in the Architecture/Engineering/Construction industry (AEC). Now that you have read *The Lion Attitude*, you have a much clearer understanding of how to move forward with your own leadership growth.

Let's walk together as you are expanding your leadership skills. I'll be with you, rooting for your success every step of the way.

To help you move forward faster on this new journey toward masterful leadership in all areas of your life, I've created a special gift for you.

The *Lion Attitude Toolkit* includes the resources I found invaluable as I was going through my own leadership reinvention. This list includes websites, useful tools, motivational speeches, and other information I used during my journey to reinvent myself, and ultimately create a training system designed to address the particular challenges of AEC leadership development.

I hope you find these resources as meaningful as I did. The toolkit will be expanded and updated as I discover even more information and ideas to help you.

Just go to www.LionAttitude.com/bonustoolkit and tell me where to send it.

Remember we are here to win together. Welcome to the lion pride!

Kirby

Made in the USA
Middletown, DE
26 August 2024

59251738R00116